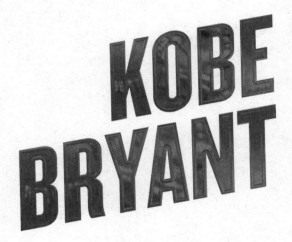

LEGENDS IN SPORTS

KOBE BRYANT

MATT CHRISTOPHER

THE #1 SPORTS SERIES FOR KIDS

WITH GLENN STOUT

Little, Brown and Company
Hachette Book Group
1290 Avenue of the Americas, New York, NY 10104
Visit us at LBYR.com
mattchristopher.com

Originally published as *On the Court with... Kobe Bryant* by Little, Brown and Company in October 2001
First Edition: January 2021

Little, Brown and Company is a division of Hachette Book Group, Inc. The Little, Brown name and logo are trademarks of Hachette Book Group, Inc.

The publisher is not responsible for websites (or their content) that are not owned by the publisher.

Matt Christopher® is a registered trademark of Matt Christopher Royalties, Inc.

Text written by Glenn Stout

Library of Congress Control Number: 2020946509

ISBNs: 978-0-316-66709-8 (pbk.), 978-0-316-66712-8 (ebook)

Printed in the United States of America

LSC-C

Printing 1, 2020

Contents

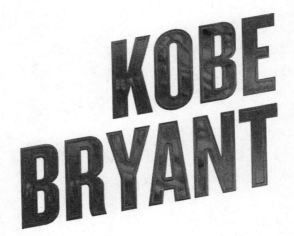

★ CHAPTER ONE ★

1978–1983

Jellybean Goes to Italy

If you look in the 1983–1984 edition of the *Official National Basketball Association Register*, you can find the complete career statistics of Joe "Jellybean" Bryant.

Nothing in the record of the six-foot-nine-and-one-half-inch, 215-pound center-forward really stands out. It states that he graduated from John Bartram High School in Philadelphia and attended LaSalle College for three years, averaging just over 20 points per game in two seasons of basketball. In 1976 he left school and was selected in the first round of the NBA draft.

From 1976 to 1983, Jellybean, who earned his nickname after some young fans gave him jellybeans following a game, played with the Philadelphia 76ers, San Diego Clippers, and Houston Rockets. He had a solid career in the NBA, averaging eight points a game and earning a reputation as a fine passer and a defensive specialist. But Bryant wasn't quite big enough to play center full-time and didn't shoot quite well enough to play forward. He was wonderfully athletic, but in some ways was ahead of his time, for his flashy style of play wasn't much appreciated in the NBA three decades ago. He was a role player who left the spotlight to teammates like future Hall-of-Famers Elvin Hayes and Julius Erving. None of his teams ever won an NBA championship, and Bryant never made an All-Star team.

Yet none of that begins to measure Joe Bryant's contribution to the NBA. For in the long run, Joe Bryant may have left a greater legacy to the NBA than many of its better-known stars.

That's because Joe Bryant is the father of the Los Angeles Lakers' Kobe Bryant, one of the youngest and brightest stars in the NBA, a player who joined the NBA directly out of high school. The son's career has eclipsed that of the father. Kobe Bryant has already been an All-Star, won the NBA Slam Dunk Contest, and won an NBA championship. His story began when his father's NBA career came to an end.

After the 1982–83 NBA season, Joe Bryant's career was at a crossroads. After eight seasons in the NBA, including three years as a starter for the Houston

Rockets, Bryant had become a second-string player. He had settled into a backup role on the Rockets, who had finished with a record of 14–68, the worst in the league.

That finish gave them the right to select seven-foot-four-inch center Ralph Sampson, the best player in college basketball, in the NBA draft. That may have been good news for Rocket fans, but it wasn't very good news for Joe Bryant. Now that they had Sampson, the Rockets didn't really need Bryant. So, at the end of the season, the Rockets released him.

No other team in the NBA expressed much interest in signing the veteran, preferring to stock their rosters with younger and cheaper players. At age twenty-eight, it appeared as if Joe's career as a professional basketball player had come to an end.

The popular Bryant probably could have gone into business in Houston, but he and his wife, Pam, also a Philadelphia native, decided to return home.

Bryant quickly discovered that he missed the game of basketball. But he didn't want to coach or anything like that. He still wanted to play.

Fortunately, Bryant was a good friend of a man named Sonny Hill. Hill ran a well-known summer league in Philadelphia and had contacts throughout the basketball world. He told Bryant about a unique opportunity to keep playing the game he loved.

Although basketball had been invented in the United States, the game had spread all over the globe and was probably the world's second most popular sport, after soccer. Several European countries even supported their own professional leagues.

Like all pro sports leagues, they were always on the lookout for talent. And the United States was still the home of the best basketball players in the world. Representatives of the Italian professional league had contacted Hill and told him they were in the market for some talented American players. They paid well and played a much shorter, easier schedule than the NBA, usually with only one game a week. Hill told Bryant he should consider playing in Italy. When Bryant said he was interested, Hill put him in touch with the Italians.

Bryant was precisely the kind of player the Italians wanted. His NBA background, size, and skills were guaranteed to make him a star in the Italian league. Moreover, his effervescent personality was certain to make him a crowd favorite. Bryant was intrigued, and not just because it meant he could keep playing basketball.

When Joe had played in the NBA, he'd spent a lot of time on the road. He sometimes went a week or more without seeing his family. Joe and Pam were the parents of three young children. Their oldest daughter, Sharia, was seven years old, sister Shaya was six, and Kobe, named after a special type of steak and born on August 23, 1978, was five. While Bryant still held out some hope of returning to the NBA, he worried about the effect such continued absences would have on his family.

The more Joe and Pam discussed the possibility of moving to Italy, the better it sounded. The money was good and the lighter schedule meant he'd be able to spend a great deal of time with his family. In addition, they thought that living in Italy and traveling around Europe would be a wonderful opportunity for their children to experience a different culture. They decided to accept the offer and move to Italy.

Kobe Bryant's basketball education was ready to begin.

★ CHAPTER TWO ★

1984–1991

His Father's Son

The Bryants packed up their belongings and moved to Rieti, Italy, in 1984. While Joe Bryant was learning the ins and outs of Italian basketball and Pam Bryant was finding her way around a new city, Sharia, Shaya, and Kobe, who had just turned six, started attending an Italian school.

Surprisingly, the Bryants' three children had a relatively easy time adjusting to their new culture. Children are adept at learning new languages. Although they didn't understand a word of Italian when they began school, as Kobe later explained, "My two sisters and I got together after school to teach each other the words we had learned. I was able to speak Italian pretty well within a few months."

Joe Bryant experienced a similarly quick transition to basketball Italian-style. On his Italian team, he was the "go-to" guy, the player who was supposed to score points and entertain the fans. He thrived in the somewhat less-competitive league. Few players could match his blend of size and quickness. He averaged over 30 points per game and wowed the crowd with dunks, long jumpers, and no-look passes. In a matter of weeks, he became one of the league's best-known and most popular stars. The fans even made up songs about him claiming he was a better player than NBA stars like Kareem Abdul-Jabbar.

The family loved their new life. They enjoyed traveling around Europe to see such sights as the Roman Colosseum in Italy and the Eiffel Tower in Paris. They also enjoyed the opportunity to experience new cultures. In much of Europe, for example, people don't buy all their food at grocery stores. Instead, they often shop at outdoor markets full of fresh fruits and vegetables. But for the Bryants, the best part of living in Europe was the fact that the entire family got to spend so much time together.

Although they faced little prejudice in Europe because of their African-American heritage, it was still difficult, particularly at first, for them to make friends. So they turned to one another for strength and company.

Kobe loved being around his father. He went to many of his games and loved seeing the way the crowd reacted to his father's spectacular play. He often played basketball with his father and his sisters, and at six years old could already dribble and shoot.

Kobe's grandparents were always sending the family packages filled with videotapes of American television shows and movies that were impossible to see in Italy. Usually, they included a large number of tapes of the NBA, which at that time was only rarely broadcast in Europe.

Kobe loved sitting with his father and watching the tapes of games. As they watched, Joe analyzed the play and explained what was happening on the court to Kobe. It was as if Kobe was attending his own private basketball school.

Of all the players Kobe watched on the tapes, his absolute favorite was guard Earvin "Magic" Johnson of the Los Angeles Lakers. The six-foot-nine Johnson led the champion Lakers, and his unique combination of skills took the game into a new era. For despite his size, Johnson played point guard and proved that skilled taller players can be just as adept at guard play as smaller men. Kobe watched the tapes of Johnson over and over again, and put pictures of the Lakers star all over his room.

Kobe's fascination with Johnson continued even

when he was playing. But although there was a basketball court at Kobe's school, he had a hard time finding other kids who wanted to play. Unfortunately for Kobe, most Italian children preferred to play soccer.

While Kobe learned to play soccer and enjoyed the game, basketball was his favorite sport. So when he couldn't talk other children into playing basketball, he played by himself.

He invented a game he called "shadow basketball," telling people later that he "played against [his] shadow." What Kobe meant was that while playing alone he learned to imagine a court full of players and played entire games against imaginary opponents. Sometimes he'd pretend he was Magic Johnson leading the Lakers' fast break, and other times he'd pretend he was his father. His ability to visualize basketball situations and then react to them would later prove invaluable to his development as a player.

But shadow basketball still wasn't like playing on a team. So Joe had Kobe join a club team.

In most of Europe, organized sports are run by clubs. A single basketball club, for instance, sponsors a number of teams, ranging from youth teams to teams of adults. Since basketball isn't a sport most Italians play while growing up, the focus is on fundamentals.

As a result, when Kobe was learning the game he spent untold hours doing drills, learning the correct way to dribble, shoot, and guard his opponent. In contrast, most American youngsters learn the game on the playground, where it is easy to pick up bad habits.

But since Kobe learned how to play the right way from the very beginning, he didn't have any bad habits. Playing club basketball, combined with watching his father and tapes of the NBA, gave him a sound foundation in the sport. Kobe never developed any bad habits that he had to break. From the time he was a child, his game was fundamentally sound.

Meanwhile, Joe Bryant was in an enviable position. He was one of the best and most popular players in Europe. Every time his contract was up, a number of teams would clamor for his services.

He switched teams several times, causing his family to move. But they didn't mind. Being together was all that mattered.

Every year they went back to Philadelphia to visit with family. Kobe loved going back to see his grandparents, and he also enjoyed the opportunity to play pickup basketball with neighborhood kids. And even though they would be in America only a few weeks, his father would sign him up for the local youth basketball league, the Sonny Hill League, so he could continue to improve and be exposed to a different style of play.

When Kobe was eleven years old, he began to grow taller. Over the course of the next two years he grew more than a foot, to over six feet tall. He towered over most of the other kids in school.

For many children, growing so fast can lead to a period of awkwardness as they adapt to their growing body. But Kobe was playing so much basketball that his coordination was able to keep pace with his growth. His game improved exponentially.

He was soon one of the best players in his club, regardless of age. He learned to dunk the basketball and could imitate many of the moves he had learned from watching the tapes and his father, and from playing shadow basketball. His friends would tease him, however, saying that while he was becoming a good European player, he "wouldn't be so good in America." Kobe tried to laugh it off, but he was beginning to suspect the same thing. He wanted to play in the NBA someday, just like his father had. But would he be good enough?

11

Joe Bryant had been paying close attention to how well Kobe was playing basketball. He was aware of his son's worries. He himself had now been playing professional basketball for sixteen seasons and he was beginning to slow down. In fact, when Kobe and Joe played one-on-one, Joe had to play hard in order to beat his son. While still a valuable player, he wasn't a big star anymore. Although he probably could have held on and kept playing for another year or two, he was financially secure. So, when Kobe was thirteen, Joe retired.

The Bryants decided that it was time to return to the United States. In the United States, Joe knew that Kobe could continue to work on his game, maybe earn a college scholarship, and, perhaps, play in the NBA. Those opportunities simply weren't available in Europe. His son needed better competition, and the entire family was ready to move on to another stage in their lives.

It was time for Kobe Bryant to go home.

⋆ CHAPTER THREE ⋆

1992

Back to America

Moving back to the United States after being away for eight years was far more difficult for Kobe than moving to Europe had been. He was older and was leaving all his friends behind. He had become comfortable living in Europe. Now, America was almost a foreign land to him.

Kobe had lived abroad for so long that he no longer spoke English very well. And many things that were familiar to most American kids, like the most popular TV shows and musical groups, were almost unknown to him. Kobe didn't have much in common with other American teenagers.

The Bryants moved to a suburb of Philadelphia, just outside the city limits. They enrolled Kobe in eighth grade at the local middle school.

At first, Kobe was overwhelmed. The school was much different and much, much bigger than the school he had attended in Italy. Although Kobe was a very good student and soon discovered that in many ways his classes were easier than they had been in Italy, he struggled with the language and initially found it hard to make friends.

He was, quite literally, caught between two worlds. As he later remembered, "That made me the odd man out from the jump." The situation was made even worse by the fact that he was going through adolescence, an awkward stage of growing up that everyone goes through. Many adolescents lose confidence and don't feel very good about themselves as they struggle to make the transition from child to adult. Kobe had particular difficulty learning how to relate to other African Americans at his school. After all, when he was living in Italy about the only African-American faces he saw were those of his parents and two sisters. Kobe hadn't had any close African-American friends since he was a little kid.

The street slang used by many of his peers was particularly hard for Kobe to understand. "Blacks have their own way of talking," he recalled later, "and I really had to learn two languages in order to fit."

His situation wasn't helped by the fact that Kobe already stood well over six feet tall and towered over many of his peers. He often found himself the butt of their pranks and jokes.

But on his very first day of school Kobe discovered that he knew a universal language that could help break down the social barriers he faced. That language was the sport of basketball.

On that first day, as Kobe sat alone in the cafeteria eating his lunch, a classmate sauntered over and stood before him, sizing him up. When Kobe realized the other young man was staring at him, he slowly raised his eyes and looked up.

"I hear you're a pretty good basketball player," said his classmate with a sneer. Word had spread rapidly that the new student with the funny accent was the son of Joe Bryant, who was still well known in Philadelphia.

Kobe tried to stay cool. He wasn't quite sure what the other student was trying to say. He just looked the boy in the eye and slowly nodded.

"Well, to be the man you have to beat the man," said the student, gesturing to himself. Now Kobe noticed that several of the young man's friends hovered nearby, awaiting his reaction.

Kobe realized that if he acted as if he was intimidated, they might give him a hard time. He knew he was being challenged, but he also knew that if there was one thing he could do, it was play basketball.

"Okay," he said confidently, "let's play." Kobe and the other young man then made arrangements to play one-on-one after school.

Word quickly spread around the school that the new kid had accepted the challenge to play the best player in the school. When Kobe got to the court there were dozens of students ringing it to watch the matchup. His challenger was already warming up and bragging to his friends about how bad he was going to beat Kobe.

Kobe didn't quite understand the attitude of his opponent, for as he later admitted, "I didn't understand the school-yard rules, the trash-talking, the machismo." But he did understand basketball. He tried to ignore his opponent's boasting and called for the ball and started to play. The crowd buzzed with anticipation.

For the next twenty minutes or so Kobe and his challenger went at each other, but in a matter of only a few minutes the outcome was obvious. Every time his opponent got the ball, Kobe was all over him, blocking his drive, sticking a hand in his face, and swiping at the ball. The other player could hardly get a shot off. When he did, it either clanged off the rim or missed the rim entirely for an air ball.

When Kobe had the ball, it was another story. He discovered he was much quicker than his opponent, had better footwork, could jump higher, and was far more skilled. For although his opponent was talented, he had learned to play on the playground and lacked the sound set of basketball fundamentals that Kobe had learned by playing on his club team in Italy, by himself, and with his father.

For example, when his opponent tried to guard him aggressively and bang him away from the basket, Kobe knew better than to try to force up a shot. Instead, he'd throw a fake, spin past him in a blur, and soar to the basket for an easy layup. When the player adjusted and backed off to prevent Kobe from driving past him, Kobe didn't try to bull his way to the hoop. Instead, he calmly drilled one jump shot after another.

The crowd soon quieted, then started cheering for Kobe as he poured the ball into the hoop over and over again. Then Kobe did something remarkable.

As his frustrated opponent came out to challenge him for the ball, Kobe faked left then drove to his right, soared through the air, and slammed the ball home.

The shocked crowd turned silent for a moment, then

erupted in cheers. Kobe Bryant, an eighth grader, had dunked the ball! As one of his friends said later, "I never saw a player like that. You just don't see guys in the eighth grade flying through the air and dunking the basketball."

A few minutes later, exhausted, his opponent gave up and the two young men shook hands. "I got my respect right there," Kobe remembered.

Although Kobe would still experience some awkward moments adjusting to his new school, he had taken an important first step. In addition to his family, basketball was the only other aspect of his life in Italy that was familiar to him in America. Even though he would occasionally have to struggle to make himself understood, he learned that basketball was a language that everyone knew.

Kobe soon found that he was welcome to play on the local playground and began making friends. At first the other players occasionally tried to test him and disrupt his game with trash talk and rough play. But Kobe quickly adjusted, not by adopting the same tactics, but by using his skills to render them ineffective. Kobe responded to trash talk by making his next shot, and he reacted to overly aggressive play by turning his game up a notch.

He also joined the eighth-grade team and quickly became the star, scoring at will. He was already looking forward to playing basketball at his local high school, Lower Merion. Their basketball team, the Aces, was one of the best teams in suburban Philadelphia and would soon finish the season with a stellar record of 20–5.

Aces coach Gregg Downer soon heard rumors about the eighth grader. Curious about him, he invited Kobe to participate in one of the Aces' practices. He figured that watching Kobe scrimmage against better, more experienced players would give him an idea of just how good Kobe was and what work he would have to do to play varsity basketball someday.

He saw a youthful, quiet, very thin thirteen-year-old amble into the gym. Nothing about the way he carried himself screamed that he was a basketball player.

He inserted Kobe into a scrimmage and sat back to watch. Within moments, he was stunned.

Kobe didn't just keep up with the varsity — he dominated them, getting off his shot with ease, stealing the ball, and rebounding. Downer's team included several players who had already won college scholarships. Yet Kobe appeared to be the best player on the floor.

Unable to believe his eyes, Downer then asked Kobe to play him one-on-one. Downer himself had played college basketball and still played in a competitive adult league. He had to see for himself if Kobe was really that good.

He was. The coach went down to a quick defeat at the hands of the student.

Downer began to look forward to having Bryant on his team. Four of the five starting players on the Aces were scheduled to graduate. Downer knew he would have to rebuild, and everyone was expecting Lower Merion to slip back in the pack. Despite their current record, the suburban school just didn't have the reputation of a basketball powerhouse.

Kobe wanted to be part of the rebuilding plan. His goal was not just to make the team, but to become a member of the starting lineup.

Very few freshmen make the varsity team in any high school sport. Most underclassmen have to play a season or two of junior varsity basketball against players of similar skill levels and experience before they can play effectively on the varsity. Basketball great Michael Jordan, for instance, was cut from his team as a freshman and didn't make the varsity until his junior year. Even fewer freshmen make the starting lineup.

But Kobe wasn't like most freshmen. He was more mature, both physically and mentally. By playing club basketball in Italy, with its focus on fundamentals and team play, he already knew how to play the game in a system. Most freshmen, despite the skills developed on the playground, have very little concept of team basketball. They have to learn to play in an entirely new way.

Kobe worked out long and hard during the off-season, adding weight training to his regimen to become stronger. As the beginning of the basketball season approached, expectations for Kobe Bryant and the Aces were high. As the son of a former NBA player who had been one of the best basketball players ever to come out of the Philadelphia area, everyone expected Kobe to be an immediate star.

In practice, Coach Downer continued to be impressed. "He's a very talented player," he told the press at the beginning of the season. "He has the ability to do everything well."

But he was also cautious with his young star. "I'm not applying a lot of pressure on him," he insisted. To help with Kobe's transition, Downer even asked Joe Bryant to serve as an assistant coach.

Kobe, who sprouted to six-foot-four at age fourteen,

easily earned a place in the starting lineup as a guard. Now all he had to do was play.

But by their opening game, it became clear that the 1992–93 season would be difficult for the Aces. Their two best returning players, center Matt Sniderland and guard Sultan Shabazz, were injured and wouldn't be able to play for the first month.

A tough schedule in the Central League, one of the best high school leagues in the state, didn't help. Time and time again the Aces stayed close only to lose in the final moments.

But Kobe was everything Downer had expected, and then some. He was often the best player on the floor, and always the youngest. Although there were times he could score at will, Downer was even more impressed by his court savvy and willingness to play in a team concept. When the opposition began double- and triple-teaming him, Bryant didn't force his shot. Instead, he looked to pass and involve his teammates in the game.

Although the Aces finished the season with a dismal 4–20 record, including 3–15 in league play, they played hard all season long and didn't give up. Bryant led the team in scoring, averaging 18 points per game, despite breaking his kneecap and missing the final games of the season.

Kobe ended the season with a new goal. He told a friend that he wanted to play in the NBA.

That goal itself was no surprise, but when Kobe planned to enter the NBA was. He told his friend he didn't want to go to college first. He wanted to go straight to the NBA from high school.

His friend just laughed. Only a handful of players had ever entered the NBA directly from high school. Even Michael Jordan hadn't been good enough to do that.

But Kobe was serious. He and his buddy made a friendly wager over Kobe's dream, which he kept a secret from his family.

But it wouldn't remain a secret for very much longer.

✦ CHAPTER FOUR ✦

1993–1995

The Ace of the Aces

When his knee healed in the spring of 1993, Kobe immediately went back to work on his game. That meant playing against his father and his uncle, John "Chubby" Cox, who had briefly played in the NBA himself. The three spent hours on the driveway court at the Bryant home.

They worked on everything — free throw shooting, dribbling, driving to the basket, and shooting. When they played one-on-one, Kobe got a chance to try out his offensive skills on a player bigger and more experienced than he was. He also had to play tough defense in order to stop his father and uncle. The competition was much more intense than playing high school basketball.

As talented as Kobe was, Joe Bryant was six-foot-nine, experienced, still in shape, and still able to provide more than enough competition for his son. In their practice sessions, he played hard, knowing that Kobe wouldn't improve if he took it easy on him. By the end of the summer Kobe was occasionally beating his father.

One time that summer Kobe blasted by his father, soared to the hoop, and laid the ball in the basket. As he turned the ball back over to his father, a wry smile formed on Kobe's face. He knew he was improving and thought his father could no longer keep up with him.

Joe Bryant noted his son's growing confidence and decided to teach him a lesson. He dribbled the ball slowly and moved in toward the basket as his son guarded him, waving his hands in the air. Then Joe Bryant saw his chance. Overconfident, Kobe had overplayed him and was just a little out of position, with his weight on his heels.

That was the only advantage a player as good as Joe Bryant needed. He swirled around his son, jumped to the hoop, and stuffed a thunderous jam through the basket. Kobe was left behind, his feet still stuck to the ground.

He realized he still had a lot to work on. "I didn't think he was that quick," Kobe said later.

When basketball season started that fall, Kobe was much improved. He'd grown another inch and was even stronger and faster than he had been the previous season. And, like his teammates, he had the added benefit of a year of experience playing basketball at the varsity level.

Downer was impressed with the improvements in Kobe's game. "He does it all," he said. "He's a very complete ballplayer and at this time he's got the total package. He doesn't have a weakness." The coach told the press he expected his team to finish the year with a record above .500, a significant turnaround.

Kobe knew that Downer would expect even more of him in his sophomore season, but he had confidence in his game. "I don't think of it as pressure," he said of the expectations that everyone had for him. "I'm young and for me it's just fun and games. I think we'll be a lot better than four and twenty."

With Kobe leading the way, the Aces were much improved. They now won many of the close contests they had lost the previous season. Kobe upped his scoring average to 22 points and also averaged ten rebounds per game. The Aces went 16–6 and made it into the second round of the Pennsylvania Interscholastic Athletic Association's state basketball tournament.

After the season Kobe continued to work on his game. Basketball became a near full-time occupation, particularly in the summer. He played in no fewer than six different summer leagues, including the prestigious Sonny Hill League, whose alumni included many players, like Joe Bryant, who had become professionals. He also attended the LaSalle College basketball camp and the ABCD camp in New Jersey, which attracted some of the best high school basketball talent in the nation. Some days, he began playing at 9:00 A.M. and didn't stop until 9:30 at night. Of his grueling schedule, Kobe said, "I just love the game. I want to play as much as I can while I can. As long as I'm happy playing, I'll play all day and all night."

Eddie Jones, a star at Temple University who later excelled in the NBA, spotted Kobe in the Hill League and befriended him. He became his unofficial escort, taking him to inner-city Philadelphia to play against the best collegiate talent in the area. Kobe fit right in, as he had learned to add schoolyard moves like the crossover dribble to his game. He was virtually unstoppable.

In his junior year at Lower Merion, everyone expected Kobe to lead the team to the league title and, possibly, the state championship. For although the Aces had lost three valuable seniors from the previous season, the remainder of the team now had the experience they had lacked in the past. As Downer said of his team, "We have plenty of talented kids besides [Bryant]. We'll be more than a one-player team."

The Aces got off to a fast start and at midseason were a stellar 11–1. Basketball fans throughout Philadelphia looked forward to their next game, which matched them with powerhouse Coatesville, one of the best teams in the state.

Coatesville had their own superstar in forward Richard Hamilton, a player many thought was even more talented than Kobe. He would later lead the University of Connecticut to an NCAA championship and play in the NBA.

The game was incredibly close. Kobe scored 16 points in the first half, but Coatesville still led at the half, 33–29. But entering the final quarter, Lower Merion nursed a one-point lead.

The teams traded the lead back and forth several times before Lower Merion pulled ahead by four points with less than a minute to play. But Coatesville didn't give up.

Trailing by two with only seconds left, Hamilton got the ball on the right side of the basket. He drove toward the hoop, then spun into the lane.

Kobe came out to stop him, but the wiry Hamilton

twisted and ducked beneath him, rolling in a layup to send the game into overtime.

Again the clubs traded the lead back and forth. Then, while trying to guard Kobe, Hamilton fouled out of the game.

But Coatesville responded to the loss of their star and led, 77–73, with less than a minute to play. It looked like the Aces were going to fall short.

Kobe patiently dribbled the ball upcourt as Coatesville scrambled to set their defense. When he was twenty-five feet from the hoop, they backed off, covering the passing lanes and blocking his way to the basket.

Kobe didn't hesitate. He launched into the air and shot.

The ball soared in a high arc and then came down.

Swish! The ball hit nothing but net and the referee threw up both his hands, signaling a three-point basket. Now Coatesville led by only one point.

Lower Merion needed to get the ball back and quickly fouled. When Coatesville missed the foul shot, Kobe swooped in and grabbed the rebound.

The crowd was roaring as Kobe dribbled downcourt and the clock ticked down. Ten . . . nine . . . eight . . .

As Kobe crossed midcourt, he picked up his pace,

cutting first to the right and then to the left, past a defender just above the free throw line as he looked for an opening.

Seven . . . six . . . five . . .

He spotted an opening between defenders and slashed into the lane.

Four . . . three . . .

As several Coatesville defenders raised their arms and swarmed over him, Kobe pulled up, jumped, and shot a soft six-footer.

Two . . .

Swish! The ball found the bottom of the net! Kobe and the Aces won, 78–77!

The big win put the Aces in position to dethrone the defending Central League champions, Ridley High. In early February, the two teams met to decide the title.

The Aces trailed by five, 51–46, entering the fourth quarter. Then Kobe took over.

In the final period he poured in 13 points and set up forward Jermaine Griffin for several easy baskets for another 12. Lower Merion won going away, 76–70. Kobe described the game later. "It was like a heavyweight fight. We would not take no for an answer." Kobe finished with a career-high 42 points.

The win clinched the league title for the Aces, and they began to look ahead to the state tournament. But in their district quarterfinal versus Norristown, Kobe played poorly at first, missing several easy shots.

The vocal Norristown crowd took notice and began to taunt Kobe, chanting, "O-ver-rat-ed." It seemed to work at first, as Kobe couldn't get his game going. At halftime, Kobe had only six points and the Aces trailed by eight, 35–27.

But in the second half he responded to the pressure like the professional he wanted to be. He scored an incredible 29 second-half points, including 18 in the fourth period. Lower Merion fought back to win, 75–70. By the end of the game the only noise from the crowd came from delirious Lower Merion fans. "It's the best feeling in the world to silence an opposing crowd," said Kobe after the game.

The Aces fought their way into the state tournament, then ran up against a tough Hazleton team. Despite Kobe's 33 points and 15 rebounds, the Aces lost, 64–59, in overtime.

Kobe was crushed. After the game he broke down in tears and apologized to his teammates for not doing more in the loss.

His teammates and coach scoffed at his apology. As

one teammate said later, "Playing with Kobe makes you play better." They all knew Kobe had done everything he could to help them win.

But Kobe Bryant was still determined to become even better. With only one year remaining in his high school career, he hadn't forgotten about his dream of playing in the NBA.

★ CHAPTER FIVE ★

1995–1996

Senior Season

One of Bryant's classmates was the daughter of Philadelphia 76ers coach John Lucas. One day in the summer before Kobe's senior year at Lower Merion, she told her father that he should see Kobe play. He did, and soon afterward invited Kobe to the gym at St. Joseph's College. When Kobe arrived, Lucas said, "I've got a surprise for you."

In walked 76ers star Jerry Stackhouse. Lucas asked him to play Kobe one-on-one. In a few moments it became clear that Kobe could keep up with the NBA star. Afterward, Lucas asked Kobe if he'd like to work out with some of the other 76ers players.

Although the 76ers didn't hold any official practices during the summer, some members of the team and other pros who lived in the Philadelphia area regularly got together at the college gym to scrimmage. Kobe jumped at Lucas's offer. It was another chance to play basketball and improve his skills.

Kobe was excited, but he wasn't nervous. Nothing about basketball made him nervous. "I had no butterflies," he said later. "No nothing. I never felt intimidated."

Few young players would have had the same response, for the group included players such as New Jersey Nets tough guy Rich Mahorn and 76ers Dana Barros, Clarence Weatherspoon, and seven-foot-six-inch center Shawn Bradley, in addition to Stackhouse.

Although many of the pros were initially skeptical about playing with a high school student, Kobe soon won them over with his play. As Mahorn said later, "He blended with the rest of us," not the best player on the court, but not the worst, either. "He even tried to 'poster' [dunk] on me," recalled Mahorn. The burly big man rejected Bryant's shot, but offered, "That's not the point. He actually tried."

They would play for hours, competing in a series of games to eleven baskets, then choosing new sides and playing again. The games were more than a test of skill. They were also a test of stamina and desire.

Kobe proved he had all three. In one memorable contest, Kobe was matched up against the 76ers' Willie Burton, an explosive offensive player who had scored a team-best 53 points in a regular-season game the previous season.

The first time down the court, Burton took the ball to Kobe and popped in a jumper over his head. As they ran back upcourt, Burton threw some trash talk Kobe's way.

Kobe didn't get mad. He got even. On defense, Kobe hounded Burton the remainder of the game, limiting him to only one more basket. On offense, he showed the veteran that he had some skills of his own, scoring every way possible — hitting long jumpers, driving to the hoop, and dunking the ball. Kobe scored ten of his team's eleven baskets as they romped to a win.

Burton stormed off the court after the game and never returned to the 76ers. The last anyone heard, he was playing in Europe.

Kobe's performance caused him to revisit the wager he had made with his friend a few years before. "After a while," said Bryant of his experience playing with the pros, "it kind of popped into my mind that I can play with these guys. I could get to the hole, I could hit the jumper, I could score, although not at will, but I could get some shots. I was able to create for my teammates and rebound. Plus, the guys respected me, and when they respect you, that must mean something."

Before the summer was over, Kobe's confidence received several more boosts. At the prestigious ABCD camp, a showcase of high school talent, he was named MVP. At the Adidas Big Time Tournament, a similar event, he earned first-team honors. Then he added another MVP title playing in Pennsylvania's Keystone Games, scoring 47 points in the final to lead his Delaware Valley Team to the title over Philadelphia. Commented Gregg Downer afterward, "Kobe's just in a league of his own, really. He just has levels of his game that no high school player has possibly ever reached."

By the time Kobe returned to school to begin his senior year, virtually every top-notch college in the country was trying to convince him to accept a scholarship. Most scouting services were calling him the best high school player in the country. But he was also attractive to colleges for another reason. Not only was he a great player, he was also a great student who carried a grade-point average above 3.0 and had scored well over 1000 on his SAT, an important test required of most students considering college. Kobe had both the athletic and academic skills to succeed in college.

Some observers expected Kobe to attend nearby LaSalle, which was Joe Bryant's alma mater and where he now served as assistant basketball coach. Many thought that LaSalle had hired Bryant just to give them an edge in recruiting Kobe.

Joe Bryant scoffed at that charge, and also dismissed any notion that he was pressuring his son to attend LaSalle. Early that fall he told the press, "I'm a father first. If I couldn't look out for Kobe's best interest, I wouldn't have taken this job." Then he tipped off the press to another possibility. "What I tell Kobe is that he can go to any college that he wants to. Yet, then, Kobe's dream has always been to play in the NBA and that dream is more a reality for him now. If that's what he wants, why should he not go?"

The father and son had already discussed the topic, and as Kobe noted at the time, "My parents raised me to be an individual, to make my own decisions, and this is my decision." It wasn't a secret anymore that Kobe Bryant wanted to go straight to the NBA. His father had become convinced that Kobe could do so after he had seen the way Kobe had played against the pros that summer. He still knew many people who worked in the NBA and knew that word of Kobe's play had filtered up to pro scouts. They were beginning to look at him as closely as the colleges were.

But the possibility that Kobe Bryant might move directly from high school to the NBA was controversial. For many years, the NBA had not allowed its teams to sign high school players. When they finally changed the rule, only a handful successfully made the transition from high school to pro basketball. They had all been big men, like Moses Malone, Darryl Dawkins, and most recently, Minnesota Timberwolves star Kevin Garnett.

But some observers thought it would be irresponsible for Joe Bryant to allow his son to skip college. They believed Kobe wasn't mature enough for pro basketball or the pro lifestyle and warned that if he failed, or lost his confidence, his career could be ruined.

Some people also thought that Joe Bryant was pressuring Kobe to play pro basketball to make up for his own disappointing NBA career. Bryant dismissed the notion. "I don't need to live my life through Kobe," he said. "I've already played in the NBA."

All those concerns would have been valid for most high school players, but Kobe was different. Growing up in Europe and around pro basketball for his entire life left him mature beyond his years. As Joe Bryant said, "Talking to Kobe isn't like talking to a seventeen-year-old. It's like talking to a twenty-three-year-old."

Kobe tried to deflect speculation over his future by talking about the present. All he wanted to do was lead Lower Merion to a state title.

He knew that wasn't going to be easy. Coach Downer had decided to challenge his team and had upgraded Lower Merion's schedule. They were due to play some of the best high school teams in the country, including the tough competition at the Beach Ball Classic, a national tournament in South Carolina. In addition, several key players had graduated and Kobe's surrounding cast would be relatively inexperienced. That would allow the opposition to double- and triple-team him every time Lower Merion had the ball.

The Aces stumbled out of the blocks. In an early-season meeting against Philadelphia powerhouse Roman Catholic High, Kobe was matched up against Donnie Carr, a player some observers considered his equal. Carr lived in the inner city and was considered to be tougher and more aggressive than Kobe, who some complained played a softer, more "suburban" game. The two had faced each other before in summer camps.

Of Kobe, Carr said disdainfully, "If he's a pro, I'm a pro."

A crowd of more than 1,500 turned out to watch the contest. They got their money's worth.

In Lower Merion's defensive scheme, Kobe had to guard Carr one-on-one. But Roman Catholic used a zone against Lower Merion, so when Carr guarded Bryant, he usually had help.

It was a close game. But Roman Catholic did a better job distributing the ball than Lower Merion. Although Bryant played well, he tired in the fourth quarter. After scoring 28 points in the first three periods, in the fourth he missed five of six shots to finish with 30 points. Meanwhile, Carr exploded for 34 and Roman Catholic won, 67–61.

A few weeks later Lower Merion faced the St. Anthony's Friars of New Jersey, a nationally ranked power. With a big game, Kobe could score his 2,000th point in high school, a landmark reached by few other players.

St. Anthony's exposed Lower Merion's lack of depth. Despite missing two starters who had been suspended for disciplinary reasons, the Friars' defense collapsed on Kobe, and the other Aces were unable to make up the difference. After Lower Merion hung close for the first three periods, the Friars pulled away in the final quarter to win going away, 62–47. Kobe scored 28 points to go over 2,000 for his career, but he found it an empty achievement. "If we won, getting two thousand would feel awfully good," he said after the game. "Now it just feels like an ordinary accomplishment."

And the Aces were playing like an ordinary team. Downer admitted they were in trouble. Unless the ball was in Kobe's hands, Lower Merion couldn't hang on to it, or score. "There are concerns," he said. "No question about it."

The Aces' dependence on Kobe was made even more apparent in the opening game of the Beach Ball Classic against Ohio's Central Catholic.

Kobe played the best game of his young career, beating Central Catholic almost by himself, as he scored 43 points on 18 of 27 shooting, including three of five from behind the three-point line, and collected 16 rebounds. On defense, he guarded six-foot-eleven standout Jason Collier and held him to only 22 points. But Kobe's teammates scored only 22 points in the 65–60 victory. Downer knew such an imbalance couldn't continue.

In their next game, against Jenks of Oklahoma, the Aces were dumped in overtime, dropping their record to 4–3. Once again, Kobe had been almost the entire show as his teammates stood around and watched him perform. After the game, Downer lit into his team.

He gave a fiery speech that he called "The Cancer of Me." He lambasted his players for not playing team basketball.

"Everything had been me, me, me," he said later. "It had to be about we, we, we."

Downer explained precisely what he expected each player to do. "We did strict role definition," he said. "I told them, 'You can shoot from here, you can shoot from there. This is what we expect of you.' I told them if they couldn't accept their roles, they could turn in their uniforms."

The only player doing what he should was Kobe, which was everything every other player wasn't. As he described it later, "My job was just to plug holes. Whatever the team needed — rebounding, scoring, passing."

Sharpshooter Dan Panagrazio became the team's designated long-range shooter, and gritty Jermaine Griffin their main rebounder. Brendan Pettit was supposed to focus on defense. Point guard Emory Dabney was responsible for getting the ball to his teammates in the right position. The Aces got the message.

They began playing as a team again, which took the pressure off Kobe and, at the same time, made him an even more potent threat as defenses had to focus at least some of their effort on other players. Panagrazio lit it up from outside and Griffin swept the glass. The Aces started blowing their opponents out.

Kobe exploded for 50 points in one 95–64 rout. After another blowout, this one an 84–56 shellacking of Germantown Academy in which Kobe scored 29 and added 17 rebounds, 6 assists, and 5 steals, the opposing coach lamented, "They were more than just Kobe." After the win, which made the Aces the first undefeated champions of the Central League, Dan Panagrazio said, "It's amazing. Kobe is not only a great individual, but he makes everyone on the court so much better. He takes us from being a good team to a great team on any night. If we keep this up into the playoffs, there's no limit."

In Kobe's final home game a week later, he took his last bow before the home crowd in spectacular fashion. After Academy Park jumped ahead, 6–4, Kobe took over, scoring the next 12 points in every way possible — three-pointers, dunks, put-backs, and drives. Lower

Merion led, 16–6, and never looked back.

Kobe finished with 50 points, matching his career high. So far, he had done everything possible in his high school career except the one thing he wanted most of all—winning a state championship.

Well, winning the state championship and then going straight into the NBA. In the next few weeks, both would be decided.

State Champs

During one practice just before the beginning of the state tournament, Coach Downer watched in wonder as Kobe took off from the foul line and jammed in a monstrous dunk. "There are no limits," he said wistfully.

Downer's summation appeared correct as the Aces knifed through the competition to reach the state semifinals with ease. But in order to reach the championship game, they would have to defeat their old nemesis Chester, regarded as perhaps the best defensive team in the state.

The previous season, Chester had embarrassed Kobe and Lower Merion, beating them by 27 points. To remind themselves of that, each member of the Aces wrote the number 27 on his basketball jersey.

Early in the game it appeared as if Chester still had Kobe's number. They swarmed over him, daring him to shoot through double- and triple-teams. Kobe began pressing, and instead of involving his teammates in the game, he tried to do everything himself. Rather than passing the ball to another player, he'd drive and try to cut between defenders and throw up spectacular-looking but incredibly difficult shots. As Kobe said later of his first-half effort, "I was making too many moves. There was too much jelly on my jam."

That style caused his teammates to become spectators. Instead of moving without the ball and trying to get themselves open, they stood around on offense and watched Kobe.

At the end of the first quarter Chester held a narrow lead. At halftime they still led, 31–29. Kobe had shot an uncharacteristic 4-for-14 from the field.

Fortunately, Kobe and his teammates had played much better on the defensive end of the floor. Although Chester had tossed up 43 shots in the first two quarters, few went unchallenged and they managed to make only 14. So far, defense had kept Lower Merion in the game, but everyone watching knew that if Kobe didn't get going in the second half, his dream of winning a state championship would go unfulfilled.

At the half Coach Downer tried to remind his players of their roles and the need to remain patient on offense. He didn't want Kobe to stop shooting, but he wanted to make sure he took his shots in the context of his team's offense.

In the third quarter, Kobe started heating up. Instead of forcing the issue, he took what the defense gave him and started pouring in shots from the outside. On defense, Lower Merion continued to contest every shot, and in the fourth quarter they pulled ahead.

Chester was becoming desperate. Nearly every time Kobe touched the ball, they fouled him. He calmly sank free throw after free throw, helping the Aces to a five-point lead with only two minutes left to play.

But Chester clawed back, tying the game at 61 with only 41 seconds remaining. Then Dan Panagrazio, Lower Merion's second-highest scorer and three-point specialist, went down with a leg injury and was forced from the game.

For the next 41 seconds, the teams went at each other hard. But as they flew up and down the court, fighting for every rebound, neither team could put the ball in the basket. The game entered overtime.

Kobe took over. The exhausted Chester defense

couldn't keep up with him anymore. With less than 20 seconds left to play and the Aces leading 75–69, the ball ended up in Kobe's hands.

He dribbled down the court and the defeated Chester team let him go. At the free throw line he left the court and launched himself into the air. Raising the ball high above his head with one hand, he took aim at the basket.

Slam! He jammed the ball home, providing an exclamation point to the Aces' well deserved, hard-fought 77–69 victory. They were going to the finals!

"We knew it was going to be a war coming in," said Kobe later. He had proven to be the best soldier on the court when it had mattered most, scoring 20 of his game-high 39 points in the fourth quarter and overtime to secure the win.

In the finals, Lower Merion faced Erie Cathedral Prep. Erie was determined not to let Kobe run wild in the final.

Erie decided to approach the game with a two-pronged strategy. On offense, they planned to slow everything down and control the tempo. That way they hoped to keep Lower Merion from running and keep the ball out of Kobe's hands on the fast break, where he was most dangerous. And when Lower Merion did get the ball, they decided to double- and triple-team Kobe, knowing that with Panagrazio still sidelined, the Aces didn't really have another scoring threat. The strategy wasn't pretty to watch, but Erie was willing to do anything to win.

The first quarter went just the way Erie had planned. Kobe went scoreless and Erie took a small lead in the low-scoring game.

Coach Downer cautioned his team to remain patient and not try to force things. They listened well, and in the second quarter Kobe managed to shake free for eight points. But the Aces shot only 6-for-22 in the first half and Erie led at halftime, 21–15.

Downer wasn't too concerned. The Aces had been taking good shots; they just hadn't fallen.

He made adjustments. "We tried to give them some different looks," Downer said after the game. "We tried to get Kobe inside and move him around. The key was to get him in transition."

Erie was taken aback by the change in strategy at the beginning of the second half. Lower Merion scored 11 straight points, only two by Kobe, as his teammates finally found their range. When the horn blew to announce the beginning of the final quarter of Kobe's high school career, Lower Merion led, 37–31.

But Erie regrouped and remained committed to their game plan. They hit a series of long jumpers and led, 41–39, with just over three minutes remaining.

Then Kobe tied the game with two free throws. He added another basket, and with just over a minute remaining, Lower Merion led, 45–43.

Now the pace of the game suddenly turned frantic as each team scrambled to score. Erie missed a jump shot and the Aces rebounded, but quickly turned the ball over.

Erie probed the Lower Merion defense, looking to tie the game. With 30 seconds left, one of their players tossed up a runner from the lane. The shot ricocheted off the rim and Kobe soared high above everyone to pull down the rebound. Just as Downer hoped, now Kobe had the ball in transition.

Kobe dribbled quickly upcourt as Erie struggled to stop him. At the top of the key, they swarmed around him. Bryant gave a little fake then flashed a pass to teammate Omar Hatcher, hitting him in full stride. Hatcher laid the ball in and Lower Merion led by four. One foul shot later, the game ended. The scoreboard told the story: Lower Merion 48, Erie 43.

When the final whistle blew, fans rushed the court and the Aces piled up on one another in a big knot. A few moments later, the players took turns mounting a ladder and snipping down the net.

Although Kobe had scored "only" 17 points, he had still been the best player on the court, a player who had made his entire team better and led them to a championship. "This is the final chapter Kobe wanted to write," said Downer. "He deserves it."

Kobe couldn't stop smiling. "Fifteen years from now we'll get together and talk about how we won the state championship," he joked. "But now, I'm gonna take a shower and party."

All joking aside, Kobe knew that now that he had accomplished his goal of winning the state title, the conversation would soon turn to another topic.

Would Kobe Bryant really decide to go straight from high school to the NBA?

★ CHAPTER SEVEN ★

1996

Decisions, Decisions

Kobe had but one short month to make up his mind. If he decided to enter the NBA draft, the league required that he declare his intentions in early May, nearly two months before the draft, which was scheduled to take place on June 26. Similarly, if he wanted to attend college he had to decide as quickly as possible because a number of schools, including LaSalle, were holding scholarships for him. It wouldn't be fair to keep them waiting forever.

In newspapers and magazines all over the country, sportswriters and various other basketball personalities debated his options. Most felt that it would be a mistake for Kobe to go straight to the NBA.

Their arguments made a great deal of sense. If he went to the NBA, most people believed he was taking a gamble. If he failed in the NBA or became injured they worried that he might never attend college and would thereby compromise his future. They claimed that attending college and experiencing the collegiate lifestyle were important for his personal development and maturity. They cautioned that if he chose to enter the NBA, he might someday regret it. There would be no turning back.

They also cited the experiences of several other young basketball phenoms who had gone straight into the NBA only to have disappointing careers. Center Darryl Dawkins, for example, had entered the NBA out of high school in 1975, becoming a teammate of Joe Bryant's on the Philadelphia 76ers. A remarkable physical talent, Dawkins had lingered on the bench for several seasons before becoming a starting player. And although he had a productive career, he never quite seemed to reach his potential. Many people thought that if Dawkins had attended college for four years he could have developed into an all-time great.

Some observers also expressed concerns about how Kobe's decision might affect other young players. While Kobe was immensely talented, other players without his myriad skills and maturity might incorrectly assume that they, too, could go straight from high school to the NBA. If they miscalculated and the NBA disagreed with their assessment of their skills, their opportunity to attend college to play basketball would be gone, for once a player declares for the draft and signs with an agent, he becomes ineligible for collegiate play. That had, in fact, already happened to several misguided players. Thinking they could go straight to the NBA, several such players didn't take the academic side of high school very seriously. But they were rejected by the NBA and then discovered they were unprepared to move on in a life without basketball.

Others in the basketball community questioned whether Kobe had the talent to make it in the NBA. At six-foot-six and just over 200 pounds, Kobe was what basketball fans sometimes refer to as a "tweener," a player without a true position. They believed that he was too small to play forward in the NBA and didn't yet have the ballhandling or shooting touch to play guard. Jon Jennings, then the director of player development for the Boston Celtics, was one of many NBA insiders who were outspoken in their belief that Kobe wasn't yet an NBA prospect. "It's a total mistake," he told a reporter.

But others believed Kobe could and should go straight to the NBA. They recognized that his background was much different from that of most high school players. They realized that he was more mature and had been exposed to pro basketball his entire life. In Bryant's defense, they cited a number of high school stars who had rejected a chance to go directly into the NBA and chose to attend college, only to be injured or have disappointing careers that harmed their professional prospects. They argued that if the NBA was interested in Kobe, he should jump at the chance and take the money he was certain to be offered. He might not get a second opportunity.

Kobe's parents spent hours discussing his decision with him. But they didn't try to sway him one way or the other. Joe Bryant best summed up their attitude toward their son by saying simply, "Kobe has choices."

Instead of pressuring him, they just tried to make sure that he was aware of the opportunities and risks that each choice entailed. Unlike many other players in his position, for Kobe the money he would earn in the NBA wasn't really an issue. The Bryants were well off and Kobe was under no pressure to join the NBA for monetary reasons.

Meanwhile, as Kobe struggled with his decision, he won a host of honors and awards. His per-game averages of 31 points, 12 rebounds, 7 assists, 4 blocks, and 4 steals during his senior year made him a consensus all-state selection in Pennsylvania, and he was named to the prestigious *Parade* and McDonald's High School All-American teams. *USA Today* even named him their High School Player of the Year.

Kobe finally reached his decision and held a press conference in the gym at Lower Merion High School just after the final bell on the afternoon of April 29. His classmates raced from class and crowded into the gym to hear the announcement. They were joined by hundreds of media members, the teaching staff, and Kobe's family.

Kobe approached the podium, his shaved head glistening, wearing his best suit jacket and a pair of trousers he'd bought at the last minute, which needed tailoring. The gym turned still as he stood and surveyed the crowd.

Most seventeen-year-olds would have been nervous, but Kobe was cool and assured. He had daydreamed about this moment for years. Before he spoke, he tilted his head, rolled his eyes, and brought his fingers to his chin as if still pondering his decision. Everyone laughed as Kobe's stunt broke the tension.

Then Kobe spoke, clearly and confidently. "I've decided to skip college and take my talent to the NBA," he said.

The gym erupted with applause. His peers had long known of his desire to go to the NBA and they wholeheartedly supported his decision. But Kobe wasn't finished.

"I know I'll have to work extra hard," he said, "and I know this is a big step, but I can do it. It's the opportunity of a lifetime. It's time to seize it while I'm young. I don't know if I can reach the stars or the moon. If I fall off the cliff, so be it." Then he stepped from the podium and embraced his parents as an informal press conference took place.

Kobe's mother reiterated the family's support of their son. "We were going to support him no matter what he chose to do. Whether it was college or the NBA, we're always going to support him. That's what we do. It was Kobe's decision."

Then she added, "With Kobe, nothing really concerns me about this decision. Like any parent, I have concerns about drugs, alcohol, and fast women, but kids are encountering that in high school.

"But Kobe is a balanced young man," she went on. "He's always stayed focused on what is really important. I don't worry with Kobe or any of my children, because we have a great family foundation."

Then Joe Bryant spoke, admitting, "Hey, I would

have liked Kobe to go to school for four years and go to Harvard. But is that reality? This was Kobe's dream. This is his life, so it was his decision."

All of a sudden, Kobe Bryant was big news. His decision to go straight to the NBA was a national story, and Kobe became instantly familiar to most professional basketball fans.

His next step before the draft was to select an agent to represent him in contract negotiations. A few weeks after his announcement, Kobe and his family traveled to New York for a much larger, glitzier press conference at the headquarters of Adidas America, the sneaker and sportswear company. He announced that he had selected the William Morris Agency to represent him, and their first act was to sign him to a multiyear endorsement contract with Adidas. "I'm very excited for this opportunity," said Kobe. "I'm one hundred and ten percent sure I made the right decision."

Adidas CEO Steve Wynne said, "We view Kobe Bryant as one of a new generation of athletes who we think will transform sports in this country. Kobe is a kid with a vision, a kid with a dream. I think his pursuit of that dream is going to be one of the most heartwarming stories in American sports over the next couple of years."

Kobe Bryant had yet to play a minute in the NBA. He didn't even know which team was going to draft him. Yet the deal was reportedly worth nearly ten million dollars. Kobe Bryant was already a millionaire before he had played a second of pro basketball.

A number of NBA teams had scouted Kobe throughout his senior year at Lower Merion, and they now redoubled their efforts. Several teams asked him to attend private workouts so they could assess his skills in a controlled setting. Playing against high school kids was one thing, but performing in a near-empty gym under the scrutiny of NBA coaches and scouts was another.

The Los Angeles Lakers were one of the teams that flew him in for a tryout. While growing up, Kobe had been a huge Lakers fan, primarily because his favorite player, Magic Johnson, had played for them.

But after Johnson announced his retirement in 1991 upon learning he had HIV, the Lakers had rarely exhibited the championship form that marked the Magic years, a fast-breaking, thrilling style of play fans called "Showtime."

NBA legend Jerry West was the Lakers president. In the 1960s he had led the Lakers to the NBA Finals six times, where they lost each time to the Boston Celtics, before finally capturing a title in 1972. As a player, West was one of the best all-around talents in the history of the league. A six-foot-four guard, West possessed a deadly outside shot, and was able to slash to the hoop, hit teammates with pinpoint passes, and collect rebounds like a big man. He was at his absolute best in pressure situations. Opponents never felt that any lead was safe as long as he was on the court, and he developed a well-deserved reputation as a player who would do anything to win. When the NBA created their red, white, and blue logo featuring a silhouetted basketball player in mid-dribble, the figure was modeled after West. The league could not have made a better choice.

But West had never faced a challenge as difficult as rebuilding the Lakers. Try as he might, he had thus far been unable to build a championship team.

Bryant intrigued West. His youth marked him as a player a team could build around, and his myriad skills reminded West of himself. Moreover, he had heard that Bryant possessed a remarkable work ethic and that the well-mannered young man wasn't likely to be a behavioral risk.

At the same time, West also had his eye on the Orlando Magic's star center, Shaquille O'Neal, who was scheduled to become a free agent. West knew that the great Lakers teams of the past had featured not only a great guard, like himself or Magic Johnson, but also a great center, like Wilt Chamberlain or Kareem Abdul-Jabbar. Perhaps, thought West, Bryant and O'Neal might one day form a similar combination that could lead the Lakers to a championship. If everything worked out, he hoped to acquire both players.

But West still wanted to see Bryant for himself. At the workout he stood on the sidelines as Bryant performed for Lakers coaches, displaying all his skills.

Near the end of the workout, they asked Bryant to play one-on-one against Lakers assistant coach and onetime NBA defensive specialist Michael Cooper.

Bryant played well against Cooper, and his performance gave West a glimpse of what he believed was the most important quality for any player to have — his heart. He could see the desire contained in Bryant's game as he relentlessly attacked the basket on offense and challenged Cooper on defense.

West was stunned by what he saw. He had heard that Bryant was good, but the workout really opened his eyes. He later said, "He was the most skilled player we've ever worked out, the kind of skill you don't see very often. He has the potential to be an All-Star."

The workout left him convinced that Bryant could be the player the Lakers needed, particularly if they were able to acquire O'Neal as well. But there was just one problem. It wasn't going to be easy for the Lakers to get either player, much less both of them. West knew he would have to outbid every team in the league for the services of O'Neal. And the Lakers were saddled with a late pick in the first round of the draft. Chances were slim that Bryant would still be available.

Although it was no secret that Bryant hoped to play for the Lakers, his desire would have little influence on who picked him in the NBA draft. His options would be few, for if he didn't sign a contract with the team that picked him, he wouldn't be able to play in the league at all. It was that simple.

On draft day Kobe was nervous. Most observers expected him to be chosen somewhere between the tenth and fifteenth picks in the first round, long before the Lakers got to select. Yet as talented as he was, most teams still considered him a "project," a player who wouldn't be able to contribute for several seasons, and most NBA teams couldn't afford to be that patient with a number-one draft pick. Kobe hoped that would allow him to slip down far enough for the Lakers to take him.

He watched nervously as the first dozen teams made their picks, selecting college stars like Allen Iverson, who could help out immediately. Then he watched NBA commissioner David Stern approach the podium at NBA draft headquarters and announce, "With the thirteenth pick of the draft the Charlotte Hornets select Kobe Bryant of Lower Merion High School."

The Charlotte Hornets?

★ CHAPTER EIGHT ★

1996–1997

Showboat or Showtime?

Coach Dave Cowens of the Charlotte Hornets had once been a star center for the Boston Celtics. Although Cowens had been smaller than most NBA big men, he was aggressive and tenacious. He had made a career by outplaying bigger men.

He had been a particular thorn in the side of the Lakers' Kareem Abdul-Jabbar. Now, by picking Bryant, Cowens had stuck it to the Lakers once again.

Kobe and his family were upset, but realized there was little they could do. It appeared as if Bryant's career would begin in Charlotte, an idea that didn't excite him very much.

That's because Cowens didn't think Bryant was ready for the NBA. After drafting him, he called Bryant "a kid," and openly questioned how much he would play. If Cowens believed that, thought Bryant, then why had he bothered drafting him in the first place?

The answer to that question soon became clear. Cowens knew that the Lakers wanted Bryant and that Bryant wanted to play for the Lakers. He also knew the Lakers were expected to make an all-out effort to sign Shaquille O'Neal, which would make current Lakers center Vlade Divac expendable. He wanted Divac and planned to use Bryant to get the player he really wanted.

It was a savvy move on Cowens's part, but a risky proposition for the Lakers. O'Neal had yet to sign with LA, and West didn't want to trade Divac until he had acquired O'Neal. But he knew if he didn't go after Bryant right away, the Hornets might well trade him elsewhere.

As a player, West had gambled many times. Now he did so again. When Cowens dangled Bryant in front of the Lakers, West couldn't resist. He traded Divac for rights to the young player.

In mid-July Bryant flew to Los Angeles to sign the standard rookie contract, worth 3.5 million dollars. At the airport, while he waited for his luggage, a stranger approached the tall young man and said, "You must be a basketball player. Who do you play for?"

Without thinking, Bryant started to answer, "Lower Merion." Then he caught himself. "I guess I'm a

Laker," he said with a smile. He liked the way that sounded.

"I'm very excited to be here," said Bryant after the signing ceremony. "It's a dream come true to come to a team like LA that has a great history. It was a team I looked up to growing up."

Jerry West was similarly delighted, but he cautioned that Bryant was unlikely to be an overnight sensation. "In five or six years the people of Los Angeles will be talking of him in very high terms. We know there will be some growing pains in the process, but we are prepared to accept this challenge."

Kobe's father, mother, and sister Shaya soon joined him in California. Joe Bryant even gave up his job at LaSalle. They realized that Kobe was only seventeen and would need a lot of support. They all moved into a house in the southern California hills. The house had a spectacular view, with the ocean on one side and the city on another. Kobe's room overlooked the Pacific Ocean. But he tried to stay focused on his goals.

"I won't be doing a lot of hanging out after the games," said Bryant. "I'll be going home to do homework and play video games and chow down on a home-cooked meal." Bryant had already made the decision to start taking college courses in business to help him manage his new fortune.

Meanwhile, Jerry West's gamble paid off. He was able to sign Shaquille O'Neal to a contract worth an incredible 123 million dollars. The Lakers had paid a stiff price, but West had acquired the two players he believed could lead the Lakers to a championship.

Bryant was still a kid who just loved to play basketball. Before training camp started, he traveled to Venice Beach, just outside LA, where some of the best pickup games in the area were played. He wanted to be ready for training camp.

But during one game in early September, he took a tumble and cracked a small bone in his left wrist. Some members of the press questioned his maturity for playing in an unorganized game.

Although the Lakers weren't thrilled with his injury, West understood, saying, "This guy will play in a Little League tournament. It doesn't bother me. He loves to play basketball and is one of the most dedicated players I have ever seen." He appreciated Bryant's unbridled passion for basketball.

Still, when training camp opened in October Bryant

was unable to play. All he could do was run and participate in drills that didn't require him to handle the ball.

Kobe took camp seriously and worked hard to fit in. Veteran Lakers were curious about the young player. He immediately impressed them with his work ethic, but his inability to participate in workouts left him far behind. He couldn't really learn the offense or determine where he fit in on the Lakers team.

With O'Neal playing center, everything was changing and the team had to learn to play a whole new way. The veteran players were more concerned with learning their roles than they were with how Bryant was adjusting.

He also didn't quite know how to behave around the veteran club. After practice, many Lakers took full advantage of their celebrity status in the city, going to clubs and hanging out together. Kobe was too young to get into most of the nightclubs and didn't care to spend his time in them, anyway. He kept to himself, stayed quiet, and tried to learn by watching.

Some members of the team thought he was aloof and didn't quite know what to make of him. Bryant knew that until he had a chance to play and demonstrate his skills, it would be hard to fit in. Besides, although he wasn't intimidated being around the other players, he was cautious about succumbing to the NBA lifestyle. His priorities began and ended with basketball.

But that didn't make him immune to the usual hazing and pranks veterans pull on rookies. At a team dinner they made Bryant sing and teased him about his friendship with the pop singer and TV actress Brandy, whom he had taken to his senior prom. They weren't trying to be mean, but Bryant was sensitive to the teasing.

Near the end of training camp his wrist finally healed and he began to get some playing time. He demonstrated confidence in his game, but also showed that he still had a lot to learn.

Bryant played the same way he had in high school. He thought nothing of going one-on-one against players of greater size and more experience, or taking the important shot. His teammates immediately nicknamed him "Showboat."

The name stung. Bryant considered himself a team player. But he was so confident that when he saw an opening, he tried to exploit it. He just wasn't accustomed to playing in a system where every other player was a legitimate option.

He had particular trouble on the defense. He often

went for the steal or after rebounds he had no chance of getting. As a result, he sometimes left his own man wide open.

That wasn't the way Lakers coach Del Harris wanted things done. He wanted Bryant to stay within the offense, work the ball inside to O'Neal, and play team defense. Although he knew Bryant would be a great player someday, Harris also knew that his job depended upon his ability to win now. He couldn't afford to wait for Bryant and really wasn't concerned with getting him playing time. He was far more occupied with the task of getting his starters to learn to play with a force like O'Neal. The club had undergone a complete changeover since the previous year and only five players remained from the 1995–96 team.

When the season started, Bryant only played during garbage time, when the Lakers were far ahead or far behind. Even then, the instant he made a mistake, Harris pulled him from the game. Kobe didn't get his first basket until the fifth game of the season.

With O'Neal at center, everyone expected the Lakers to win immediately, and in fact they did get off to a hot start. That made it even more difficult for Bryant to get meaningful minutes. Harris was far more concerned with giving his key players more time playing with one another than he was with working Bryant into the lineup.

Bryant tried to be philosophical about it, telling the press, "My father keeps telling me my time will come." But for a basketball junkie like Bryant, sitting on the bench was hard to deal with. Some members of the press who had thought it was a mistake for Bryant to skip college took note of his lack of playing time and began whispering, "I told you so."

Behind the scenes, Lakers president Jerry West was putting some pressure on Harris to play Bryant more often, but the coach was resistant. The Lakers were on pace to win more than 50 games, and he didn't want to risk disrupting his team just to give Bryant some experience.

When the league broke to celebrate the annual All-Star weekend, the Lakers led the Pacific Division. Due more to his name than his numbers, Bryant was selected to participate in the Rookie All-Star Game; a showcase for younger players played the day before the All-Star Game.

Bryant was pumped up about finally playing. The game would be broadcast nationally, giving many NBA fans their first real look at Bryant.

In the free-form, 30-minute contest, which more

resembled a pickup game than a regular-season NBA contest, Bryant flourished, outscoring more heralded rookies like Allen Iverson to lead all scorers with 31 points.

But he saved the best for the slam-dunk contest. Although the contest had once attracted the game's biggest stars, they had begun to shy away. As a result, young players like Bryant were invited to participate.

He started slowly and barely made it to the final round of four players. Then Bryant rose to the occasion. As he had done so many times in his high school career, he saved the best for last.

Starting on the left side, he charged the basket, went into the air, and seemed to hang in defiance of gravity. As he did, he passed the ball from one hand to the other *between his legs*, then spun to the basket and slammed the ball home! It was a spectacular move.

The crowd jumped to its feet, as did judge Julius Erving, who as a player had been best known for his artistic dunking style. Jazzed up by the crowd, Bryant bounced to midcourt, stood before the judges, and flexed his slender body like a bodybuilder.

The crowd roared again. To no one's surprise, Bryant won the contest.

But none of his All-Star weekend success mattered when the regular season resumed. Bryant continued to play only five or ten minutes a game even as O'Neal was lost for over a month to injury.

But another injury finally gave him a chance to play. He began to realize he could provide some instant offense. He ended up averaging 15 minutes per game. Point guard Nick Van Exel went down and shooting guard Derek Fisher took over the point. Harris had little choice but to pair Bryant in the backcourt with Fisher.

For the first time all year, Lakers fans got a glimpse of the future. The team won five of the six games he started. Bryant proved that he could score — and the opposition discovered that at times they had to double-team him. Even better, he demonstrated that he was learning what to do in such situations, as he rarely forced a hot and proved adept at finding the open man.

Although he went back to the bench when Van Exel returned, Bryant's playing time increased as Harris began to realize he could provide some instant offense. He ended up averaging 15 minutes per game over the course of the season. O'Neal returned to the lineup and the Lakers made the playoffs easily, finishing 56–26, just a game behind the Seattle SuperSonics for second place in the Pacific Division.

In the first round, the Lakers blew out the Portland Trail Blazers, winning the best-of-five playoff three games to one. Bryant hardly played in the three Lakers wins, but in Game 3, with the Lakers trailing, he had come off the bench to keep things close by scoring 22.

In the next round, against the Utah Jazz, the Lakers lost the first two games of the best-of-five series and again Bryant played only a few minutes. But opportunity came in Game 3 once again.

The Lakers jumped ahead early, but turned cold as Utah began to make a move in the fourth quarter. Harris recalled Bryant's performance against Portland and he put him in the lineup, looking for some points.

Bryant proved he was becoming an explosive scorer. He scored 17 points in the final period as he kept the pressure on Utah by driving to the basket again and again. They responded with fouls, and he coolly sank 13 of 14 free throws to secure the 104–84 win.

If LA didn't win Game 4, their season was over.

Harris decided to go with the hot hand and Bryant played much of the game.

With the Lakers nursing an 87–85 lead with less than a minute remaining, Jazz veteran guard John Stockton went one-on-one against Bryant. When the rookie went for a fake, Stockton blew past him to score a layup and tie the game with 11 seconds remaining.

LA called time-out. O'Neal had fouled out and the Lakers needed someone to take the final shot. Harris decided that someone would be Bryant. He told his team to get him the ball and get out of the way. The decision showed a lot of confidence in the rookie.

LA inbounded the ball to Kobe and his teammates scattered, leaving him isolated on one side of the court. He moved toward the basket, pulled up, and from fourteen feet shot a potentially game-winning jumper. He had made the same shot thousands of times while playing shadow ball.

But this time, there was a national television audience, thousands of fans in the stands, and a hand in his face. The ball fell short. Air ball! The game entered overtime.

Bryant was uncharacteristically unnerved. In the extra

period he shot three more times, and three more times he missed the basket entirely. The Jazz won going away, and the partisan Utah crowd hooted Bryant and his teammates off the court.

The press questioned Harris's decision to put the ball in Bryant's hands in crunch time, and the coach snapped, "All year I get criticized for not playing him and now I'm criticized for playing him."

But no one felt worse than Kobe Bryant did. After returning to Los Angeles, the next morning Bryant went to the gym and began working on his second season in the NBA. His rookie year was over.

★ CHAPTER NINE ★

1997–1998

One Step at a Time

Bryant knew he had to work harder if he was ever to achieve the level of success he expected from himself in the NBA. In addition to his time spent in the gym, he added a grueling weight-training regimen to his fitness routine so he could become bigger and stronger. He also played for the team the Lakers sponsored in the LA Summer Pro League, coached by former player Larry Drew.

Although Bryant's performance in the playoffs seemed to indicate that he would play a key role on the team in the upcoming season, as he played in the summer league it became apparent that wasn't necessarily the case. The Lakers tried to put restrictions on his game. They didn't want him to score as much as they wanted him to pass.

Bryant tried to adjust, but he found the transition difficult. He was convinced that his talents were best used as a scorer, but the Lakers offense was increasingly focused on getting the ball to O'Neal inside. It was a slowdown style that Bryant felt uncomfortable with.

He tried his best to fit in. But in the preseason it became clear that Coach Harris planned to use Bryant off the bench as a sixth man, either at shooting guard or small forward.

While Bryant was disappointed that he wasn't in the starting lineup, the role suited him. Since he was no longer playing the point, he wasn't expected to distribute the ball. And he often entered the game while either O'Neal or the Lakers' other main scoring option, Eddie Jones, was taking a breather. Bryant's job was to energize the team and put the ball in the basket.

That was something he was beginning to do in ever more spectacular fashion. He'd grown an inch and become stronger in the off-season, and his offensive skills began drawing comparisons to Michael Jordan. He looked even taller, as he let his hair grow out into a distinctive, short Afro.

In one amazing sequence, Bryant showed that he had skills that perhaps even Jordan didn't have. In a preseason game against Washington, Bryant got the ball in transition and charged down the court, freeing himself from his defender with a nifty crossover dribble.

He had two options. He could either shoot the short twelve- to fourteen-foot jump shot or drive to the basket, where Washington's six-foot-nine forward Ben Wallace stood blocking his way.

The situation was not unlike that which he had faced at the end of the game against Utah. All summer long he had replayed the sequence in his head, trying to figure out why he had missed the shot. He finally came to the conclusion that he had shot an air ball because he had really wanted to drive straight to the basket. He hadn't because he had worried about committing a foul or being accused of being too flashy. In short, he had talked himself out of doing what came naturally, out of being Kobe Bryant. That lack of confidence had probably led to the three air balls he had shot in overtime, as well.

He was determined not to let that happen again. Without hesitation he went right at Wallace.

The big man was in perfect position — in a slight crouch in case he had to jump up to block a shot, with his arms and legs spread wide to keep Bryant from cutting past him. There was no apparent opening to the basket for Kobe Bryant.

But that didn't stop him. He took the ball in his hand, took a quick, hard step, and went up . . .

. . . and up, and up, and up. Legs spread wide, Bryant went straight at, then over, the befuddled defender, who ducked slightly as Bryant soared over his head and jammed the ball through the hoop!

His teammates, the opposition, and the fans sat stunned in their seats for a moment. Then, as the crowd roared, Bryant's teammates looked incredulously at one another. The sheepish Wallace spun and looked around as if wondering where Bryant had gone. But he was already back down to earth, racing down the court. It was a move that no one, not even Michael Jordan, could have made.

When the regular season started, the Lakers opened with a rush, winning their first eleven games. O'Neal dominated the inside and Bryant came off the bench to score almost at will, averaging nearly 20 points a game, a remarkable total for a player who was usually on the court for only half the game. While some observers groused that he was still out of control and still failed to play within the team concept, the results were undeniable. The Lakers were winning.

The comparisons to Jordan continued when the Lakers and Bulls met for the first time that season in a game the press hyped as a meeting of the past and future of the NBA. Although Chicago won by 20 and

Jordan poured in 36 points, Bryant held his own against the legendary star, hitting for a career-high 33 points and making Jordan work for every shot.

Basketball fans throughout the country were beginning to realize what Bryant's teammates already knew; he was becoming the most exciting player in the NBA. "He amazes me," said teammate Nick Van Exel. "I see him every day and he still amazes me."

Added Eddie Jones, "Every play, you look at him and you wonder, 'What's next?' I would pay money just to watch Kobe play for ten seconds."

The fans confirmed Jones's estimation of Bryant when they voted for the NBA All-Star team. Kobe Bryant, the sixth man on his own team, collected more votes than any other player, outpolling even Michael Jordan to earn a starting berth on the Western Conference squad. It was an unprecedented achievement for a nineteen-year-old player.

Although a few members of the press sniped that Bryant didn't deserve the honor, the other All-Stars were well aware that his popularity was good for the league and they welcomed him.

The game was held in New York's Madison Square Garden, smack in the middle of the world's media capital, guaranteeing that every move Bryant made would be scrutinized. Not many nineteen-year-olds could handle that much pressure, but Bryant tried to remain cool, although even he had to admit at a press conference before the game, "My body's numb, my heart's racing."

Observers were again touting the game as a matchup between Jordan and Bryant. The two players realized that's what the fans wanted to see and tried to play up to the hype.

It helped that in All-Star Games teams play little defense. In such a setting, Bryant's and Jordan's skills were on full display. The two players raced up and down the court, matching each other with shot after spectacular shot.

One shot Bryant made in the third quarter still has fans talking. The West had the ball on a fast break, and Kobe led the charge down the court.

He could have passed to a teammate, and perhaps he should have, but instead he chose to give the crowd their money's worth. He decided to take the shot himself.

In full stride he first hid the ball behind his back with his left hand as he looked the opposite way, then took it out and jumped, out of control and tumbling, at the same time before tossing up a crazy, no-look hook shot over his head, an impossible shot that somehow went in.

But that was the end of the show. Western Conference coach George Karl pulled Bryant from the game in the fourth quarter in favor of some veteran players. Bryant ended up with 18 points and 6 rebounds in 22 minutes of play against the NBA's best. But Jordan, who played most of the game and scored 23 points, earned MVP honors for the victorious East.

Bryant didn't mind. "I just wanted to sit back, observe the whole thing," he said, adding, "This is the most fun I've ever had. I'm kind of sad it's over."

Those words would prove to be prophetic, for the first weeks of the second half of the season weren't much fun for either Kobe Bryant or the Lakers. Illness and injury sent the Lakers into a slide, and after his All-Star performance, Bryant suddenly found himself the object of increased attention by opposing defenses. His shooting suffered, and he seemed to be forcing his game and appeared out of sync. Coach Harris began turning to other options on his bench and Bryant's playing time dropped. Instead of being called on to provide instant offense, he was being used primarily for his defense.

The team managed to right itself in the final six weeks of the season, winning twenty-two of their final twenty-five to finish with a record of 61–21, just a game behind the Utah Jazz and Chicago Bulls for the best record in the league. But while the Lakers thrived, Bryant withdrew, and the player who appeared on the verge of becoming the best in the game at midseason was on the verge of disappearing.

People began to openly wonder whether the Lakers were actually a better team without Bryant. In the first round of the playoffs, against Portland, he played sporadically, getting a handful of minutes in one game, then playing nearly all of the next. The Lakers won easily to advance to the next round, versus Seattle.

Bryant played even less against Seattle, getting little more than garbage time as the Lakers again swept to victory. It appeared as if the team might have an appointment with the Bulls in the Finals.

But the Utah Jazz got in the way. They exposed the Lakers on defense, as their highly disciplined offense, keyed by Karl Malone and John Stockton, ran the Lakers ragged. And on defense the Jazz, unlike most other teams, didn't just focus on O'Neal. They pressured everyone, and the Lakers simply couldn't score.

In limited time, Bryant was no more successful than his teammates.

By the time of their final defeat in the four-game sweep, the Lakers were sniping at one another and at Coach Harris. Bryant had withdrawn during the second half of the season and hardly knew what to think anymore. As he later admitted, "I've been humbled."

His future would depend upon how he reacted to that experience.

☆ CHAPTER TEN ☆

1998–1999

The Lost Season

When a reporter asked Bryant how he planned to spend his off-season, he responded simply, "Basketball. That's all."

Unfortunately, much of his work was in vain. The 1998–99 NBA season was a disaster from the very beginning. The players' union's contract with the owners had expired and the owners enforced a "lockout." When it finally ended in January, the Lakers were in disarray, out of shape, and unprepared. The result was turmoil.

Practices were a mess. Bryant was accustomed to playing hard and went all out, an approach that angered many of his teammates, who felt he was trying to show them up. During one two-on-two session with O'Neal, Corie Blount, and Derek Fisher, O'Neal and Bryant had a confrontation that resulted in a brief scuffle. Although the altercation took place because each player was tired at the end of the long scrimmage, it revealed a problem between the two. While neither player cared to talk about it, observers hinted that O'Neal was jealous of Bryant's tendency to take over on offense, which he felt left him out far too often and cost him shots. Bryant, on the other hand, thought that O'Neal's work ethic didn't match his incredible physical skills. In short, neither player really respected the other.

O'Neal and Bryant stopped talking and people wondered if it would ever be possible for the two stars to learn to play with each other. If they didn't, they would never win a championship together.

The ill feeling between the two spilled over into the regular season, as did the Lakers' disorganized play. In reality, both players were at fault, for each had always been the focus of every team he had played on. Added to that was the fact that at age nineteen, Bryant didn't have much in common with his teammates, who went out together after the game and forged friendships off the court. Bryant's best friends were still members of his own family and old friends from high school.

The club got off to a rocky start, and after only eleven games Del Harris was fired and replaced by the controversial forward and master rebounder

Dennis Rodman. Although Rodman was incredibly valuable on the court, his flamboyant life-style had often been a distraction.

But the changes made little difference, and after another twelve games the Lakers decided to retool, trading Eddie Jones and Elden Campbell to Charlotte for long-range shooter Glen Rice and forward J. R. Reid. Then Rodman, in a dizzying week of controversy, retired, unretired, and was released. Some pundits suggested the team install a revolving door leading to the locker room.

The team split into several cliques, each of which blamed the others for the club's erratic performance. O'Neal still wanted the offense to revolve around him, and Rice had a hard time adjusting to a system where he was usually the second or third option. In Charlotte, he had been his team's go-to guy, the player who got the ball at crunch time. In Los Angeles, that player was O'Neal.

Bryant felt frustrated. He thought the Lakers offense held him back and kept him from playing his game and using all his skills.

On the court, the team's internal troubles became obvious. Everyone was still trying to learn what was expected of him, but they weren't really playing together. When the Lakers struggled or the offense broke down, Bryant looked to score, which only increased the feeling of friction on the team. Too often, Bryant had the ball twenty or twenty-five feet from the basket, juking and faking and dribbling while his teammates just stood around unsure of what he was going to do next. And when Coach Kurt Rambis tried to initiate some changes in the club's offense to accommodate both O'Neal and Bryant, the team often ignored him.

But even as the club continued to struggle, Bryant's playing time increased. He moved into the starting lineup, splitting time between the guard and forward positions. As he got the opportunity to play, he cut loose and wowed fans at LA's Great Western Forum with his stunning athleticism and leaping ability. Bryant often played to the crowd, trying to top each spectacular shot with an even better one.

It was entertaining, but did nothing to help team chemistry. O'Neal and other veteran players felt left out, and Bryant was estranged from his teammates. The local media went wild reporting on the Lakers' ongoing soap opera, as O'Neal intimated that he thought Bryant alone was the cause of the team's problems. After each game or practice, Bryant went one way and the rest of the team went another. In an understatement, Joe Bryant said, "It's been a difficult year for my son."

Yet somehow, despite everything, the Lakers had enough talent to win more than they lost. But critics noted that the Lakers didn't appear to have a coherent plan on offense. When their jump shots fell, which opened up the inside for O'Neal, they won. But when they didn't, the opposition could double-team O'Neal and pick off rebounds, often holding the Lakers to just a single shot. When that happened, the Lakers had a hard time scoring and usually lost.

Bryant finished the regular season with a scoring average of nearly 20 points per game. Los Angeles faced the Houston Rockets, a team in even more disarray than the Lakers, in the first round of the playoffs.

In the first two games of the series, the Lakers looked like a team that had finally learned to play together. Bryant shut down Rockets star Scottie Pippen, and the Lakers swept the first two games.

But when Bryant got in foul trouble in Game 3, Pippen went wild, scoring 37 points as the Rockets won. Then the Lakers pulled a surprise in Game 4.

Bryant and O'Neal spent much of the first half

passing to each other for easy baskets, and the Lakers jumped out way ahead and won with ease, eliminating the Rockets. It was the way it was supposed to be, and gave everyone a glimpse of just how good the Lakers could be if O'Neal and Bryant learned to play together, just as Jerry West had once learned to play with Wilt Chamberlain, and Magic Johnson with Kareem Abdul-Jabbar.

"All those stories about me and Shaq, you can throw in the garbage," said Bryant afterward. "Look at us. We play great together."

The victory sent the Lakers up against the San Antonio Spurs in the next round. With their twin towers of Tim Duncan and David Robinson, the Spurs had the manpower to match up against O'Neal under the basket. When they did, the Lakers appeared confused. Rice and Bryant both reacted by trying to go one-on-one in an attempt to generate some offense. But the Spurs continued to dominate play underneath the basket and control the tempo of the game.

With O'Neal in constant foul trouble and the rest of the team shooting poorly, the Lakers battled hard but couldn't manage to overcome the Spurs. And for the second straight year Kobe Bryant missed several important shots late in close games, including two bricks from the free throw line that cost his team a chance to win Game 3. The Spurs defeated the Lakers in four straight games. The season was over.

Finally.

⋆ CHAPTER ELEVEN ⋆

1999–2000

Triangle Turnaround

It was obvious to everyone that the Lakers needed to change something if they were ever going to reach their potential. Some observers speculated that either O'Neal or Bryant would be traded. Or perhaps both players would be shipped off and the Lakers would embark on a total rebuilding program.

But Jerry West still believed the Lakers had all the players in place to win a championship. What they needed was someone to get it all to work together.

As coach of the Chicago Bulls, Phil Jackson had developed a reputation as a man who could get talented players with big egos to play together. For the Bulls, despite the presence of Michael Jordan, hadn't managed to win a championship until Jackson became coach.

He had installed an offense known as the triangle, a strategy that took advantage of both Jordan's skills and those of star forward Scottie Pippen. As a result, he had gotten the most from each player.

The triangle was new to pro basketball. Traditionally, most offenses had been designed to isolate a particular player one-on-one. As a team moved the ball across half-court, players set up in specific positions on the court and the point guard, out on top, called out the play and put it in motion, usually by a pass to another player. But if the defense broke up the play or it was disrupted for another reason, the player with the ball usually had few options. The ball was sent back out and another play was called. The role of each player was strictly defined.

But the triangle was different. Simply put, it demanded that the players react to what the defense did, depending on the motion and movement of each player. Each player had to be able to read the defense, learn how to react, and pass to the open man.

Although the offense was demanding, it wasn't rigid. There was plenty of room for creativity. When it worked, the ball zipped back and forth and players ran and cut all over the floor until someone worked free and finished the play, usually with a wide-open jump shot or a layup or dunk from in close. It allowed the individual player to flourish and stay involved.

Jordan and the Bulls had worked the offense to perfection. But that hadn't been the only key to their success.

Jackson's personality was much different from that of most NBA coaches. He viewed the game of basketball in human terms and appreciated it for its capacity to bring individuals together in pursuit of a common goal. While many had first scoffed at his approach, his record of success in Chicago was undeniable.

After Michael Jordan had retired, Jackson had resigned and sat out the 1998–99 season. Now he was ready to return to coaching. He let the Lakers know he wanted to come to Los Angeles. In Bryant and O'Neal, he saw two players he believed would thrive in the triangle, for each could both pass the ball and score. West believed that if anyone could get O'Neal and Bryant to work together, it was Jackson, so he named Jackson coach.

Critics questioned the hiring, saying that the only reason Jackson had been so successful in Chicago was because Michael Jordan was a member of the Bulls. Getting the Lakers to play together, they argued, would be an entirely different challenge.

But O'Neal and Bryant, for all their differences,

were actually quite similar. Each had been expected to be a star since entering the league, and each had been something of a disappointment. Both players were still referred to in terms of their potential, as if neither had yet reached it.

At the same time, they shared a common goal. Each wanted to win very badly. Their reputations had taken a beating and each player knew that the only way to silence his critics would be to win a championship. It helped immeasurably that Jackson already had the respect of both players. After all, his record spoke for itself. And Bryant and O'Neal had been dissatisfied with Harris and Rambis, neither of whom had been able to enforce any team discipline. This had led each player to feel that he needed to take over on the court, a major cause of the friction between the two. Under Jackson, Bryant and O'Neal hoped, things would be different.

During training camp each player deferred to Coach Jackson. When the rest of the Lakers saw how intent Bryant and O'Neal were on giving their new coach some respect, they fell in line. They listened patiently as he explained their roles in the triangle, and they accepted criticism each time he stopped play and explained what someone had done wrong.

As Jackson explained to his players, "I have to tell you about a mistake so you know you made a mistake. But it's not personal criticism."

Bryant thrived under Jackson's instruction, saying later that Jackson's approach had allowed him to realize when he was making mistakes without being told. Now, he said, "I know when I mess up and I say, 'OK, hold on, I've got to step back.'"

To everyone's surprise, by the time the regular season opened the Lakers were running the triangle as if they had been doing so for years. O'Neal had never been more dominant under the basket, as the offense prevented defenses from packing in around him. When he got the ball in the low post the defense was usually still in transition, allowing him an open route to the basket that often resulted in monstrous dunks. At times he was simply unstoppable, scoring at will and ripping down rebound after rebound.

At the same time, Bryant had never played with so much control. His speed, quickness, and ballhandling skills were perfectly suited for the constant motion required by the triangle. It freed him on the outside for jump shots, for drives to the basket, and, significantly, to make crowd-pleasing passes not seen on the Lakers since Magic Johnson had been a star. For the first time, Bryant began to be recognized not just for his scoring ability, but for his ability to create shots for other players.

Yet the offense still allowed him an outlet for his creative urges. He'd often find himself wide open with a clear path to the lane, the perfect situation to throw down one of his spectacular jams. Basketball had become fun again.

Before the season was a month old, it was obvious that the Lakers would be the team to beat for the NBA championship. The controversy and frustrations of the previous season melted away. O'Neal and Bryant developed a healthy respect for each other and even became friends. On one occasion, when Bryant got involved in a scuffle with New York Knick Chris Childs and elbowed him in the face, O'Neal was outspoken in his defense, saying, "Everyone knows Kobe's a clean-cut kid. He was protecting himself."

It was "Showtime" in Los Angeles again. The Lakers romped to the Pacific Division title with the league's best record, 67–15. O'Neal was named to the All-NBA first team, and Kobe Bryant made the second team, as well as the All-Defensive first team.

The team's performance earned them home-court advantage throughout the playoffs. They put it to good use as they surged to the Finals, beating the Sacramento Kings, Phoenix Suns, and Portland Trail Blazers in succession to earn the right to play the Indiana Pacers for the NBA championship.

The Pacers were tough, experienced, and talented. Under their coach, former NBA great Larry Bird, they had been knocking on the door of the NBA championship for several seasons, only to fall just short. Led by guard Reggie Miller, they were a rugged defensive team known for their clutch shooting and never-say-die attitude. Although the Lakers were favored to win, some thought the Pacers might just pull off an upset. Bird had announced he would retire after the season, and the Pacers wanted to send their coach out a winner.

But the Lakers sent a message in Game 1. Working the triangle to perfection, they fed the ball to Shaq over and over again and he came up big, scoring 43 points and pulling down 19 rebounds. "When he gets in that kind of groove," said Bryant, "you've got to get the ball to him." The Lakers won, 104–87.

In game 2, LA got off to another quick start, playing great team basketball. Bryant didn't attempt his first shot, a seventeen-foot jumper, until there were only three minutes left in the first quarter. He went up high as the Pacers' Jalen Rose jumped up to try to block his shot.

Bryant was too quick and got his shot off clean. But as it soared through the hoop for two points, he came back down to earth and his right foot landed on Rose's foot. Bryant's foot turned grotesquely and he fell hard, a wince on his face. He got back up and tried to shake off the injury, but left the game a few moments later with a badly sprained ankle.

Fortunately, Glen Rice took up the scoring slack and Brian Shaw stepped in for Bryant and led LA to a 111–104 victory. But with Bryant's status for Game 3 unclear, Rice spoke for everyone after the game when he said, "When you lose a key player, one of the things you have to do is come together collectively. We may well be short again. Guys have to step up again."

Bryant was crushed by the injury and did everything he could to prepare for Game 3, but was unable to play. Without him, the Lakers lost, 100–91. Suddenly, the Pacers seemed poised to take control of the series.

Few people expected Bryant to play in Game 4. He tried the ankle in practice but found it was still too sore. Many observers expected him to miss the remainder of the Finals.

An hour before Game 4, Bryant was still receiving treatment from team doctors. Although there was little danger he would hurt his foot more by playing on it, he was still in significant pain.

But when Bryant took the court before the game, his adrenaline started pumping and the ankle, heavily taped, began to feel better. He told Jackson he could play, and the coach put him in the starting lineup. The Lakers knew they couldn't let the Pacers tie the series.

The two teams played each other even, neither giving in. When Shaq missed a short jump hook at the buzzer, the game was tied, 104–104; it was going to overtime.

Bryant's ankle hadn't been much of a factor thus far. He'd played well, but during time-outs could be seen noticeably limping. Now he had to play extra time.

Just a few minutes into overtime, the Lakers received a severe blow. Battling for a rebound, O'Neal was called for his sixth foul and had to leave the game.

Lakers fans groaned. O'Neal had been playing a great game and his loss gave the Pacers a huge advantage.

But as O'Neal trudged to the bench, Kobe Bryant

approached him, winked, and whispered something. As Bryant said later, "This is the game you dream about as you're growing up. You lose yourself in the moment. You're consumed by the game."

Coach Jackson sensed the time for LA to win was now. He later said, "I broke down our offense and went to an open-floor game for Kobe."

Indiana immediately went on the attack. Their center, Rik Smits, hit a jump hook to draw the Pacers to within one of LA, 112–111. Then Bryant got the ball.

He never thought about his late misses in the playoffs in the past. He drove down the court, stopped, stutter-stepped, and faked a drive. Then, as the defense reacted, he stepped back to give himself some room and calmly took a jump shot.

Swish! Nothing but net! The Lakers led, 114–111.

But Smits responded with another jump hook. Once again, the Lakers gave the ball to Bryant.

The Pacers must not have believed his earlier basket, because they gave Bryant some room to shoot again. Once more he stutter-stepped, faked, stepped back, and . . .

Swish! Nothing but net again. Lakers 116, Pacers

113. "I just relaxed like I was in my backyard," Bryant said later.

The Pacers then answered with two free throws by Miller. But as the Pacer defense blanketed Bryant, Brian Shaw put back a miss by Rice to make the score 118–115. Then Smits hit two free throws to bring the Pacers back to within one at 118–117.

The Lakers had the ball with 28 seconds left. They tried to work down the clock. Forced to act before the 24-second clock ran out, Brian Shaw put up a shot.

It bounced off the rim.

Out of nowhere, Bryant flashed in, grabbed the rebound, and put it back to give the Lakers a 120–117 lead. The Pacers managed to sink a free throw in the final seconds, but Bryant and the Lakers came out on top, 120–118.

After the game, everyone wanted to talk about Kobe Bryant. "Kobe smelled it at the end of the game," said Coach Jackson, "and he lifted us."

"That was big-time tonight," added Glen Rice. "He stepped up like a veteran. That just goes to show how much he's matured." A reporter then asked Shaq what Bryant had said when he had approached him

103

after he'd fouled out in overtime. The big center smiled. "He said, 'Don't worry about it, I got it.'" That he certainly did. "That's what a one-two punch can do for you," he added. "When you injure your left hand, the right will step up and knock out the opponent."

Bryant even impressed Pacers coach Larry Bird, who had been one of the greatest clutch players in NBA history during his career with the Boston Celtics. "It was awesome," said Bird of Bryant's performance. "Every shot was all net," he said of Bryant's 28 points on 14 of 27 shooting from the field. "We knew Kobe was going to take over. It's just that we couldn't stop him."

Down three games to one, the Pacers didn't fold, winning Game 5 in a rout, 120–87. But in Game 6, the Lakers wouldn't be denied.

Behind O'Neal and Bryant, they won, 116–111, to capture the NBA championship.

Bryant scored 26 points in the finale, including four critical free throws in the final 13 seconds. At the final buzzer, he and O'Neal embraced. The victory answered forever the question of whether the two stars could learn to play together.

★ CHAPTER TWELVE ★

2000–2002

"Back to Back to Back"

Kobe Bryant had proven himself a clutch player during the 2000 NBA Championships. When Shaq was troubled with injuries at the start of the 2000–2001 season, Kobe stepped up his play again. In November, he chalked up five consecutive games of thirty or more points. He earned Player of the Month honors in December thanks to his averages of 32.3 points, 4.8 rebounds, and 4.9 assists. A month later he had his first triple-double with 26 points, 11 rebounds, and 11 assists; he added another later in the season, as well as eight double-doubles.

Overall, the Lakers were having another good run, too. Shaq recovered and returned to the lineup, and while there were times that he and Kobe disagreed, for the most part they were in sync—and that partnership helped the team to their second consecutive playoffs. Los Angeles quickly dispatched the first three teams they faced, sweeping first Portland, then Sacramento, and finally San Antonio, to reach the Finals against the Philadelphia 76ers.

The Lakers were hungry to repeat their previous year's victory, but they were dealt a blow in the first game when they lost to the Sixers, 107–101, in overtime. But that loss only served to whet their appetites. They took the next four games away from Philadelphia to win their second title in two years.

"We did it again!" Bryant cried after the fourth victory sealed their championship. Then he added, "We're going to get another one next year. Back to back to back!"

But the possibility of a three-peat was by no means certain for the 2001–2002 Lakers. While they had started the season off strong by winning 16 of their first 17 contests, midway through the schedule they dropped to second place behind the Sacramento Kings. The two teams raced neck-and-neck throughout the remainder of the season and then met for a final showdown in the semifinals of the playoffs.

The Lakers took the first game, 106 to 99; Kobe accounted for 30 of LA's points that night. The Kings fought back to win the next two, however, and then the teams traded victories—unbelievably close matches won by a single point each—to put the series at Kings 3, Lakers 2. If Sacramento won the next match, they would be going to the Finals. The Lakers, on the other hand, needed two wins to advance.

They got them. In Game 6, Shaq and Kobe combined for a total of 72 points to push their team ahead and tie the series. In Game 7, the Lakers powered past the Kings in an edge-of-the-seat overtime that ended with Bryant draining two from the line to make the final score a decisive 112 to 106.

The Championship Series wasn't quite as exciting as the semifinals. But if you were a Laker or a Lakers fan, it was plenty satisfying. Los Angeles faced the New Jersey Nets in four games and beat them in each meeting. O'Neal was the star of the series and earned the MVP Award, but Bryant did his part by averaging 26.8 points per game and 5.3 assists. His best performance came in the final minutes of Game 3, when he hit two vital jump shots to preserve his team's four-point lead.

Los Angeles celebrated their home team's three-peat with a victory parade. At the parade's end, Kobe took a turn at the podium in front of Staples Center.

"I told you all last year we're going back to back to back," he said, his happy voice echoing as confetti flew through the air and cheers rose from the crowd of 150,000 fans. "We'll be back next year. See you next year!"

★ CHAPTER THIRTEEN ★

2002–2005

10,000 and Beyond

Anticipation for yet another stellar season was high in the wake of the Lakers' three-peat. But unfortunately, some of the team's top players, including Shaq, were sidelined early with injuries and penalties. Indeed, if not for Kobe Bryant, the Lakers might have faded into the background in the fall of 2002.

But Bryant wasn't about to let that happen. Now entering his seventh season with the NBA, he was one of the most dominating players on the court, and this year his deadly accuracy from the floor became even more threatening. In one game, he nailed 12 three-point shots, a new NBA high mark. He also posted a record-tying 8 three-pointers in a single half; had a nine-game streak of 40 or more points, tying Michael Jordan's record; and a 13-game streak of 35 or more points, making him only the fourth person to achieve that benchmark. But the highlight of his sea-son came on March 5, 2003.

That night, the Lakers were playing the Pacers in Indiana. In the third quarter, Bryant got the ball and sailed into the air for a hanging jump shot. The ball slipped into the net for two points. On the surface, it wasn't a remarkable play—nothing more than what he had done hundreds of times before.

But in fact, when that ball dropped through the hoop, Kobe Bryant made history. Those two points brought his career total to 10,000, making him the youngest player in NBA history to reach that milestone.

Moments later, the crowd learned what he had done. They erupted with cheers and gave him a standing ovation.

"I really can't grasp what it means right now," Bryant said later. "I had no idea the crowd was going to stand up the way they did. It was a little embarrassing, but it was a good feeling."

Bryant continued to feel good and, along with Shaq and the other Lakers, to play great for the rest of the season. Los Angeles ended with a 50-32 record, good enough to put them in the playoffs for the fourth year in a row. They dispatched their competition there and reached the semifinals, where they faced the San

Antonio Spurs. After four games, the series was tied at two apiece.

Game 5 was a hard-fought battle that found the Lakers down by three in the final seconds. Unbelievably, they nearly sent the game into over-time when Robert Horry tossed up a three-pointer with 4.3 seconds left on the clock. The ball bounced in, and then inexplicably bounced out of the hoop. The Spurs took that game, and the next as well—and for the first time in the new millennium, the Lakers were out of the Championships.

The following year, Bryant posted numbers that were slightly lower than the previous year's. Still, his stats were outstanding: with a per-game average of 24 points, 5.5 rebounds, and 5.1 assists, he was among the top players in the league. Following his sixth straight appearance at the All-Star Game, he added his ninth career triple-double, with 25 points, 14 rebounds, and 10 assists, in a game against the Washington Wizards.

Los Angeles roared into the playoffs again in 2004 by winning 14 of their last 17 games. They then charged past the Houston Rockets, the San Antonio Spurs, and the Minnesota Timberwolves to face the

Detroit Pistons in the Finals. Once there, however, they seemed to run out of steam. The Pistons outplayed and outshot the Lakers four out of the five contests. In Game 3, they embarrassed the LA team by beating them by a 20-point margin!

In years past, such a loss would have been unthinkable. But that loss wasn't the only one the Lakers would suffer. In the following season, they took to the courts with a big hole in their roster. After eight amazing seasons, Shaquille O'Neal had been traded to the Miami Heat. Rumors swirled that the change had come at his request, made after Phil Jackson announced his decision not to return as the Lakers' coach in the fall of 2004. Others claimed Shaq was tired of competing with Kobe. Still others said Kobe pushed Shaq out, a rumor that gained momentum when his new seven-year, $136.4 million contract was announced.

In the end, however, the reasons didn't matter so much as the result—Shaq was gone. Competitors even when they were teammates, Kobe and Shaq would now be in true competition whenever they met on the court.

Fans looked forward to their first meeting, slated

for Christmas Day, with great eagerness. The media hyped the event for weeks; when the Heat and the Lakers took to the court, it was before a record-setting audience.

By all accounts, the Kobe-Shaq duel lived up to its hype. Shaq and the Heat won the game in overtime, with Shaq posting a double-double with 24 points and 11 rebounds. But Shaq also fouled out, his last two penalties given when he tried to block Kobe's drives to the hoop. Kobe, meanwhile, drained in a game-high 42 points and nearly won the game for the Lakers with a close-but-no-cigar three-pointer at the overtime buzzer.

"I had a pretty good look," Bryant said of that last shot, "but I didn't get the balance I would have liked."

In the weeks following that ballyhooed match, Kobe and the Lakers often found themselves off-balance. On January 13, Bryant suffered a severe sprain to his right ankle, an injury that sidelined him for a month. Then, midway through his recovery, head coach Rudy Tomjanovich announced that he was stepping down for health reasons. Assistant coach Frank Hamblen worked his team as best he could, but in the end, his leadership couldn't overcome the problems the Lakers were having. The season ended with LA missing a berth in the playoffs for the first time since 1994.

Kobe Bryant was disappointed with the results but had one high point to look back on. In the season's final game, he chalked up his 14,000th point, surpassing Michael Jordan as the youngest player to reach that benchmark. Still, he would have traded that milestone for a chance to win another championship ring.

⋆ CHAPTER FOURTEEN ⋆

2005–2006

81 and "The Shot"

Kobe Bryant worked out throughout the off-season to improve his speed and agility. When he returned to the court at the start of the 2005–2006 season, it was obvious to everyone that his efforts had paid off. He scored 20 or more points in six of the eight preseason games, and then exploded in the first regular-season games, posting nine games with 30 or more points, including two with more than 40! And on December 20, he was nearly unstoppable as he made shot after shot for 62 points, his best-ever game.

But even Kobe couldn't have anticipated what would happen on January 22, 2006. That night, the Lakers faced the Toronto Raptors in Los Angeles. Two minutes into the game, Bryant made a reverse layup for two points. Thirty seconds later, he added two more on a fadeaway. He didn't score again for four minutes, but by the end of the first period he had earned 14 points, four of which came from free throws. Good numbers, but not unusual for him and not enough to help the Lakers overcome the Raptors' seven-point lead.

By halftime, he had a total of 26 points and seemed on his way to yet another 40-or-more point game. Then came the second half.

After missing two jump shots in the opening minutes, Bryant hit eight in a row, including three three-pointers! He added another point with a free throw to bring his game total to 44—and then proceeded to sink virtually ever shot in the remainder of the game. When the dust finally settled, Bryant had made a grand total of 81 points!

"Not even in my dreams," Kobe said of his amazing achievement. "This was something that just happened. It is tough to explain. It is just one of those things."

That total of 81 points included 7 three-pointers and was second only to the individual all-time high score of 100, made by Wilt Chamberlain in 1962. Not surprisingly, the Lakers took the game, 122 to 104.

They took enough additional games in the remainder of the season to push them into the playoffs, too. Kobe had several more 40-plus point games and two 50-plus games during the final months.

Then came the first round of the playoffs, against the Phoenix Suns. The Lakers dropped the opening game, 107 to 102, then took the next three to go ahead three games to one. The most remarkable play during those games came from Kobe Bryant in the final seconds of the third game.

The Lakers were behind by two points. With the shot clock at 0.4, teammate Smush Parker got the ball. He passed it to Bryant. With seven-tenths of a second left, Bryant drove to the hoop and laid the ball up.

Swish!

The ball dropped, the buzzer sounded, and the game was tied! Overtime!

"It was the most fun shot I've ever hit," Bryant later commented.

And it wasn't the last game-saver he made that night. As the overtime wound down into the final seconds, Los Angeles trailed Phoenix by one. When the Suns' Steve Nash got possession of the ball, the game seemed over. Then, incredibly, Laker Luke Walton stole the ball!

Once again, Kobe Bryant was the go-to man. As the clock ticked down to the final second, he tossed up a jumper from seventeen feet away. It hit! The Lakers won, 99–98.

Los Angeles was up three games to one in a series marked by its rough-and-tumble play. They needed only one more to eliminate the Suns. They didn't get it.

Instead, Phoenix annihilated them, winning the final three games—the last by a margin of 31 points! Kobe delivered a disappointing performance that outing, adding only a single point in the second half and shooting only three times.

"They stepped up to the challenge and kept coming at us in waves," he said after the elimination. "We just didn't have enough in the tank to hold on."

Still, Kobe had much to celebrate at the end of his tenth NBA season. He had his best-ever points-per-game average, with 35.4, making him the league leader in that category. He had six 50-or-better point games, including his amazing 81-point game. Thanks to "the Shot"—the overtime buzzer-beater that handed the Lakers the win in Game 4 of the 2006 playoffs—he had a place in basketball film history.

As gratifying as such moments were, however, they meant nothing to Bryant unless they factored into the greatest moment of all: victory in the NBA Finals.

That was a moment that had eluded Kobe since 2002. It was one he wanted to relive again—soon.

But would the 2006–2007 season give him what he longed for, or would it end in disappointment as the previous four had?

★ CHAPTER FIFTEEN ★

2006–2007

Chasing the Championship

Soon after the 2006 postseason ended, Kobe Bryant underwent surgery to correct problems with his right knee. He was still recovering from the operation when the Lakers' regular season began on October 31. He watched from the sidelines as his team beat the Phoenix Suns, 114–106, and then won again the next night against the Golden State Warriors. Two nights later, he rejoined the starting lineup.

When he first took to the floor, spectators noticed a difference even before he touched a basketball. His jersey number was no longer number 8; it was number 24, his original number in high school. His reasons for making the switch were never clear, but some believed it was his way of acknowledging that he was entering a new phase of his career, one that saw him passing as much as shooting.

The next thing watchful observers saw was that the knee surgery had been a success. While he wasn't the team's high scorer—that honor went to Lamar Odom—he did drain 23 points, rip down 4 rebounds, and help out with 6 assists in the 118–112 win over the Seattle SuperSonics. Sure, it wasn't his best game ever, but it *felt* good to Bryant.

"In the first half I jumped off the leg for a reverse layup," he said later. "That was something I didn't do at all last year."

What also felt good was the fact that the Lakers won ten of their first fifteen games. The last of those, a 132–102 pasting of the Utah Jazz, saw Kobe exploding for a high of 52 points!

Bryant and the Lakers continued to play well through the rest of 2006, although Kobe was forced to sit out one game early in December after spraining his right ankle. The injury didn't slow him down that much, however. Three times that month, he posted games of 40 or more points. He was undoubtedly pleased to have performed so well—and just as undoubtedly would have wished the final results of those games were better, for two of the three ended in losses.

Fortunately, Los Angeles was winning more than they were losing. Going into 2007, their record stood at 20 wins, 11 losses. Bryant was the team's scoring machine, but other Lakers were equally important. Twenty-year-old center Andrew Bynum was steadily improving under the basket. Small forward Luke Walton regularly posted double digits in points and high figures in rebounds and assists, as did point guard Smush Parker. Under the rehired Phil Jackson's careful coaching, the team appeared to be moving ahead at full steam.

Kobe had another terrific month in January. With the exception of one single-digit-scoring game early on, he chalked up 20-, 30-, and 40-plus point totals night after night. Those points added up to yet another milestone for the superstar. On January 26, 2007, he tossed in his 18,000th point. At 28 years, 156 days old, he beat out Wilt Chamberlain and Michael Jordan to become the youngest player ever to reach that number.

"It's always special," Bryant said of the achievement. "Things like that really don't sink in until the end of your career."

But not every game was to find Bryant earning top marks for his playing. Two nights after hitting that milestone, he hit something else—another player.

The game was between Los Angeles and San Antonio. Late in the fourth quarter, the Lakers had a nine-point lead. But as the clock ticked down, they saw that lead dwindle as the Spurs' Manu Ginóbili swished 2 three-pointers and his teammates added four more. The Lakers responded with five of their own, but the Spurs matched them point for point, until the score was tied at 80 apiece.

Then, with 2.7 seconds left on the clock, Bryant got his hands on the ball 20 feet from the hoop. He drew up and jumped for the game-winning shot.

Manu Ginóbili jumped too. As Kobe released the ball, Manu blocked the shot. At the same moment, Kobe's arm slashed in an odd motion. His elbow caught Manu right in the face!

When Kobe's shot missed, the game went into overtime. The Spurs eventually won, 96–94. Kobe was disappointed at the outcome. But that disappointment was nothing compared to what he felt two days later. That's when league officials ruled that Kobe's elbow motion was "unnatural"; in their view, he had hit Ginóbili on purpose.

Bryant vehemently denied that he had meant to hurt his opponent. But it didn't make a difference. He was suspended for one game.

"I'm surprised. Shocked by it, actually," Bryant said. "You unintentionally catch people with elbows every once in a while."

Interestingly, Kobe connected with two other players with similar arm motions later in the season. The first also resulted in a single game suspension. The second was ruled a flagrant foul. Whether Bryant had meant any or all of the blows remains unclear, but regrettably, those incidents made some people consider him a dirty player.

If Bryant was having his share of problems, so too were the Lakers. After a promising start to the season, they suddenly went into a tailspin. February saw them losing six games in a row. In March, they were defeated seven consecutive times, including one game that found them losing by 36 points! By the end of that month, their record stood at 38–34.

Kobe was doing everything he could to get his team back on top. In one stretch at the end of March, he became the second player in NBA history after Wilt Chamberlain to post point totals of 50 or more in four consecutive games, with 65, 50, 60, and 50. All those games were wins for the Lakers.

Other times, such as the match on April 2, he backed off from the basket and worked on helping his teammates rack up the points instead.

"I like seeing my teammates being in a rhythm. I like seeing their confidence. I like seeing them smile," Bryant said after that night's 126–103 victory over the Sacramento Kings.

The next game, it was Kobe who was smiling. Halfway into the third quarter, he sank a free throw to make his 26th point of the game. To his surprise, the crowd erupted in cheers.

"I didn't know what the people were clapping about until I got in the trainer's room," he said later. What he didn't realize was that that shot brought his career total to 19,000 points, boosting him over Michael Jordan as the youngest player to reach that mark!

The Lakers finished out their regular season schedule two weeks later. Kobe's final point average of 31.6 was the highest in the NBA, the second year in a row he was the league's top scorer. He was proud of the achievement, as well as the fact that with ten 50-plus point games he had tied Wilt Chamberlain's single-season record.

But of course, those records didn't add up to the ultimate goal: another NBA championship.

With a record of 40 wins and 42 losses, the Lakers just squeaked into the playoffs. Their opponents? The Phoenix Suns.

The Suns had beaten the Lakers ten times in their last twelve regular season meetings. In the previous year's postseason, the Lakers had jumped ahead in the first round three games to one, only to be routed by the Suns in the final three games. This year, Los Angeles hoped the results would be much different.

They weren't. The Suns took the first game 95–87. They took the second by an even bigger margin, 126–98. The third game—a 45-point, 6-rebound, 6-assist effort by Kobe Bryant—ended in the Lakers' only victory of the series. Phoenix rode roughshod over Los Angeles in the final two matches to advance to the next round.

Soon after the final loss, Kobe Bryant made a public plea to the Lakers' front office. The team was solid, but changes to the roster needed to be made if they were to regain their championship status. "Do it and do it now," he said, adding that he was "beyond frustration" with the year's results.

He didn't know it then, but things were about to get much, much worse.

★ CHAPTER SIXTEEN ★

2007–2008

MVP?

On Tuesday, May 29, 2007, the *Philadelphia Inquirer* published a report about Kobe Bryant and the Lakers. The article quoted an anonymous source inside the Los Angeles organization as saying that "it was Bryant's insistence on getting away from Shaquille O'Neal [in 2004]" that ultimately led to Shaq being traded.

When Kobe learned of the article, he was infuriated. The reason why was simple: the source was dead wrong. The next day, he set the record straight by doing an interview with radio personality Stephen A. Smith.

Bryant told listeners of a meeting he'd had with team owner Dr. Jerry Buss midway through the 2004 season. The meeting was between Buss and Bryant only and included some news that shocked Bryant.

"I am not going to re-sign Shaq," Buss said. He believed Shaq was too expensive and too old. Then he reassured Bryant that the decision had nothing to do with the supposed feud between the two players. "This is my decision. It's independent of you. My mind is made up."

According to Kobe, Buss also stated that he planned to focus the team's efforts around Bryant, and that he wasn't thinking of rebuilding. That latter statement proved to be false, for in the years afterward, rebuilding is just what the team had set out to do.

Kobe had never told anyone of this meeting mainly because he didn't want to add to the media's obsession with the troubles between himself and Shaq. But when the 2007 article appeared, he felt he had no choice but to come forward with the real story—a story that Shaq himself said he believed one hundred percent.

Smith must have heard the bitterness in Kobe's voice in the interview for he took the conversation in a new direction. "What are your feelings about the Los Angeles Lakers organization right now?" Smith asked.

Kobe answered by saying how much he had always loved the Lakers as a kid growing up and as a player. But now he felt he had been betrayed.

"I just don't see how you can rebuild that trust," he

said wearily. "I just don't know how you can move forward in that type of situation."

"Are you saying . . . that you want to be traded?" Smith asked.

Kobe didn't hesitate with his answer. "Yeah, I would like to be traded, yeah."

That reply sent shock waves through the basketball world. Bryant was barraged with questions from reporters. At times, he seemed to back away from his statement; other times, he seemed to confirm it. In the end, one message came through loud and clear: Kobe wanted to remain a Laker, but unless the organization was willing to make some changes, he would go.

Rumors of trade talks circulated wildly in the following weeks. The Los Angeles Clippers and the Chicago Bulls were the teams most often mentioned. But by midsummer, the story had begun to fade. Kobe himself said that he had put it out of his mind in order to focus on his play for Team USA and their drive to qualify for the 2008 Summer Olympics. With Kobe setting the pace, the squad reached that goal by winning the qualifying tournament in Las Vegas on September 2.

Then it was on to the Lakers' preseason—and the

rumor mill began pumping out speculation about a Bryant trade once again. Dr. Buss added to those rumors by saying in mid-October that he would listen to any offers for his star player. But as nothing came of such talk, Kobe remained with Los Angeles.

The preseason found Bryant plagued with other difficulties besides trade talks. He had been bothered with tendonitis in his knee, for one thing. Then, a week before the regular season began, he was forced to the sidelines with a wrist injury.

The wrist healed quickly, however, and Kobe was cleared to play in the team's opening-day game against the Houston Rockets. He was loudly booed by the home crowd when he first took to the floor. But he quickly turned those jeers into cheers with an amazing 45-point performance. Those points added up to almost half the team's total score. Unfortunately for Lakers fans, that total was two less than the points racked up by the Rockets.

Los Angeles played Phoenix in their next outing— and embarrassed the team that had embarrassed them in the playoffs by winning 119–98. That game, Kobe demonstrated his new role of team facilitator, or the player who spurs on the action with crisp passes, able assists, aggressive rebounds, and pinpoint shooting.

For his efforts, he posted 16 points, 11 rebounds, 4 assists, and 3 steals in 28 minutes of play.

By the end of November, the Lakers had a record of 9–7. It was not their best showing in years, but it was respectable nonetheless. By the year's end, they had bettered it to 19–11. Those wins included a December 23 match that saw Kobe Bryant earning an early Christmas present.

That night, the Los Angeles Lakers played the New York Knicks in Madison Square Garden. The Lakers jumped to an early lead, and by halftime were ahead 55–37. Kobe had drained 17 of those points, including 2 three-pointers. Then, in the first minute of the third quarter, he hit another three-pointer.

All of a sudden, the crowd erupted with cheers. With that shot, Bryant had made his 20,000th career point! He was the thirty-first player to reach that mark and the youngest in NBA history. The Lakers won the game, thanks in large part to Kobe's 39 points, 11 rebounds, and 8 assists.

Less than a month later, Kobe closed in on another historic record in a thrilling game against the Seattle SuperSonics that was decided in the final four seconds of overtime. The score was tied at 121 points apiece when Bryant got the ball 18 feet from the basket. He turned, shot, and *swish*! Two points and the win!

Those points brought his game total to 48, his first 40-plus game of the season—and the 87th of his career. If he had just one more game with more than 40 points, he would tie Elgin Baylor, who had 88, for third place in the NBA record books. Few people doubted he would tie and eventually surpass Baylor, and soon. And that's exactly what happened.

On January 25, 2008, he reached 88. On February 1, he made it 89. Nineteen days later, he was up to 90—despite pain in his right pinky, which he had dislocated earlier in the month. On March 2, he posted his 91st 40-plus game with a 52-point effort, his highest point total so far that season. And before March was through, he bested *that* mark by draining 53 points for his 92nd 40-plus game—and his 23rd 50-plus career game!

Such performances had some people whispering that this year, Kobe Bryant would finally win an award that had eluded him so far in his career. Despite posting fantastic numbers in most of his eleven seasons, Bryant had never been voted the NBA's Most Valuable Player.

No one disputed the fact that Kobe was a great player, perhaps the best on the court. The trouble was, many were uncertain if he was the best *team* player. For those voting for MVP, this is what the award represented.

That Kobe himself recognized this fact became clear in a reply he gave in mid-April when asked if he thought he had a chance to win.

"The MVP nowadays is not an individual award, you really have to make your teammates better and elevate your ball club. I think for me to be nominated in that race is a tremendous honor because that's really been one of the criticisms people have had of me, how well I make my teammates better. From that standpoint, I feel like I have already won."

But were his efforts enough for him to win MVP votes? Only time would tell. Meanwhile, he still had a job to do—namely, help the Lakers win their way through the playoffs and into the Finals!

On April 11, the Lakers clinched first place in the Pacific Division of the Western Conference with a nail-biting 107–104 win over the dangerous New Orleans Hornets. Two nights later they beat the reigning NBA champions, the San Antonio Spurs, by a walloping 106–85 to jump ahead to first place in the Western Conference.

"It's all about momentum," Kobe commented.

That momentum carried the Lakers through their last regular season game, a 124–101 blowout over the Sacramento Kings. Kobe had 20 points that night, most of which were free throws. He also had 5 assists. The second of these marked yet another important milestone in his career.

Bryant entered the game with 3,998 total career assists in eleven seasons. Within the first minutes of the first quarter, he had added number 3,999. Then, with 7:22 showing on the game clock, he dished the ball to teammate Vladimir Radmanović, who drove in for a layup. Radmanović added two points to the Lakers' score—and Kobe became the sixteenth player in NBA history to have 4,000 career assists, only the third Laker to reach that mark.

Kobe was pleased to have earned his way into the top ranks of basketball players. But there were still two goals that eluded him, the MVP award and a fourth NBA championship title.

That the Lakers could achieve the second of the two was possible, for Los Angeles swept the Denver Nuggets in the first round of the playoffs to advance to the Conference Semifinals versus the Utah Jazz. Kobe played one of the best games of his life in that first round. He hit 18 of 27 shots from the floor, made 5 out of 9 three-pointers, and added 8 more points on free throws for a total of 49 that night. He also contributed 10 assists; in all, his performance accounted for 69 points of the team's total score!

It was efforts like that that made it easy for sportswriters and broadcasters to decide on the 2007–2008 MVP. On May 6, they chose Bryant in a landslide that saw him garnering 82 out of 126 first-place votes.

Kobe was thrilled to finally receive the award that had danced just out of reach for so long. But he didn't claim the trophy for himself alone. He knew that he wouldn't be holding it if it wasn't for his teammates.

"This is really a brotherhood. We're really, really close, all of us," he stated on his website. "We're brothers, man."

Now all that remained to be seen was whether that brotherhood could power their way through the playoffs and win the ultimate prize: the NBA Championship.

★ CHAPTER SEVENTEEN ★

2008

Nightmare and Redemption

The Los Angeles Lakers had disposed of the Denver Nuggets in four straight games. The Utah Jazz didn't fold as easily. After the Lakers won the first two games, the Jazz fought back to tie the series at two apiece. Game 5 was played in Los Angeles before a screaming, celebrity-filled crowd, a crowd whose loyalty to the boys in purple and gold was rewarded with a win.

The Lakers needed just one more victory to advance to the Conference Finals. They got it the next game, thanks in large part to Kobe Bryant, who helped crush a Utah rally by draining 12 points in the last quarter. "We want to keep it rolling," Bryant said of his team's momentum. "It's a great accomplishment to get to the Conference Finals, but we believe we can accomplish much more." So far, the Lakers were 8–2 in the playoffs. Two games later, against their conference opponents, the San Antonio Spurs, their postseason record was 10–2.

Those wins hadn't come easily, however. The first, in fact, nearly went to the Spurs, who had a 20-point lead midway through the third quarter. Up until then, Kobe had taken just three shots, only one of which had made it through the hoop.

Considering that he hadn't scored less than 22 points in the previous ten outings, some wondered if his hot hand had cooled off. It hadn't. Four minutes into the third quarter, he hit a jump shot. Two and a half minutes later, he hit another, and followed that with an assist to teammate Pau Gasol—his sixth assist of the night. After that came a three-pointer and two free throws, then two more assists to Gasol. He finished the quarter with yet another bucket and one more assist to bring his point total to 13, with 9 assists.

The final quarter started with the Spurs ahead, 72 to 65. One minute later, it was 72–67 thanks to Kobe's driving layup. The Spurs got two free throws to widen the gap again, only to see it close on a jump shot from Bryant. It got tighter just minutes later, when number 24 made back-to-back buckets to bring Los Angeles within three points of tying the game. Would they have enough muscle to draw even in the time they had left?

They would! With 3:18 showing on the clock, Lamar Odom rolled in a layup off his fingertips to tie it up at 81 apiece. Seconds later, Bryant was fouled. He hit both free throws to give the Lakers their first lead of the game, and then sweetened the deal with a jump shot.

The Spurs weren't about to sit back and let LA roll over them, however. Manu Ginóbili sank two free throws. Then Tim Duncan tossed in a jumper to tie it at 85 to 85. As the clock ticked down, an overtime decision seemed inevitable to many. But not to Kobe Bryant!

With less than thirty seconds remaining, he brought the ball to the lane, drew up, and lofted a ten-foot jumper that arced over the Spurs' outstretched fingers and into the hoop. The Lakers had a two-point lead, and when a teammate hit two free throws moments later, that lead stretched to four. From a onetime 20-point deficit, the Lakers had surged to take the game, 89–85. The following game wasn't nearly as exciting, but it was rewarding—for Lakers fans, anyway, who saw their team win by a margin of thirty points, 101 to 71.

Kobe and the Lakers took care of business in the next two games, a victory that saw Kobe scoring 17 of his 39 points in Game 5 in the fourth quarter. "We're all extremely excited," Bryant said after the win that pushed them into the Finals. "Now, it's time to go on and see if we can't finish it off."

"Finishing it off" wouldn't be a simple task. To win the NBA Championship, the Lakers would have to beat the strongest team in the league, the Boston Celtics, who made it to the Finals for the first time since 1986. They were led by the Big Three: forwards Paul Pierce and Kevin Garnett and guard Ray Allen.

The media was in a frenzy over the Lakers–Celtics matchup. The teams were traditional rivals, and had previously met in the Finals nine different times, with the Celtics winning eight of those matchups. But Kobe Bryant had never faced the Celtics in a Final. Lakers fans hoped he would be the difference.

Game 1 was played in Boston, where the Celtics were virtually unstoppable on their home court, and Boston took the game 98 to 88. They seemed certain to win the next game, too. With only eight minutes left in the third quarter, the Lakers were down by 24 points.

But Los Angeles hadn't reached the Finals by

giving up. Kobe led the comeback. Early in the first minute of the fourth quarter, Bryant ripped down a defensive rebound and dished it to teammate Jordan Farmer, who tossed in a three-pointer. Kobe assisted on the next four points, too, then he tried his hand at shooting. A 19-foot jump shot failed to fall, but the 18-footer he attempted next swished the strings on its way through the hoop. He then added two free throws after standing his ground and drawing the offensive foul. As the clock was winding down, he dished off for a three-pointer. Kobe now had had a hand in 14 of the last 16 points made by the Lakers! And he wasn't done yet. Another assist led to three more points by Derek Fisher. Then Kobe hit a three-pointer of his own, followed in quick succession by back-to-back running jump shots. When teammates Sasha Vujačić and Vladimir Radmanović added five points with a three-pointer and a dunk, the Lakers were suddenly within four points. Then, with less than a minute to go, Kobe was fouled. He lined up for his free throws and made them both! Those two points brought the Lakers' twelve-minute total to 41. Unfortunately, those two points were the last the team made that game, and Boston held on to win.

The series moved to Los Angeles for Game 3,

where the Lakers squeaked out an 87–81 victory. It appeared as if the Lakers would tie the series in Game 4 only to have the Celtics, down by 24 midway through the second quarter, make one of the most dramatic comebacks in NBA postseason history to win 97–91. Even in defeat, Kobe Bryant had been the consummate team player that game, dishing 10 assists, nabbing 4 rebounds, and sneaking 4 steals. Unfortunately, the Celtics had shut him down on offense. He ended the night with just 19 points, all in the second half. "They were determined not to let me beat them tonight," Kobe commented later. "I saw three, four bodies every time I touched the ball."

The Lakers were unable to recover from the defeat and although they won Game 5 103–98, back in Boston the Celtics thrashed the Lakers 131–92 to take the title.

Bryant was bitterly disappointed with the final out-come. During a postgame press conference, he was asked about the future of the team, and whether he planned to be part of that future. He gave a simple three-word answer: "I don't know."

"I'm upset more than anything," he admitted later. "Frustrated...Understand that second place just means you're the first loser." And yet, underneath that disappointment was another equally strong feeling about his team. "I'm proud. I'm proud of my guys. I'm proud of the effort that we gave." Still, in the back of his mind he knew that, with Shaq long gone, now the Lakers were considered his team. Until he proved that he could lead them to a championship, some would still doubt him as both a player and a leader.

A short time later, he spoke to NBA legend Michael Jordan and expressed his frustration at the loss. "You got all the tools. You gotta figure out how to get these guys to that next level to win that championship," Jordan told him.

Kobe didn't wait very long to start figuring it out. Soon after the Finals, he began to practice with the 2008 United States Olympic team for his first Olympic appearance.

Although the United States had traditionally dominated Olympic basketball, four years earlier, in 2004, with a team of younger, less experienced players like Allen Iverson, Stephon Marbury, and nineteen-year-old LeBron James, the USA turned in a disappointing performance. They failed to play as a team and only won a bronze medal. Afterward, USA Basketball decided to take no chances. In 2005, they recruited the best players in the NBA to play, and asked them to commit to the team in the off-season for the next three years.

Kobe was one of the first players asked to join. Although he was not much older than many of his teammates, he had something many of them did not: championship experience. From the start, team chairman Jerry Colangelo and coach Mike Krzyzewski let Kobe know how important he was to the team. They didn't need him to lead in scoring. They wanted him to make sure they played as a team and made it to the next level.

Kobe listened and took great pride in playing for his country. "You can play for the Los Angeles Lakers, you can play for the Spurs, the Heat, the Mavs, whoever," he said, "but it's different when you put on a USA jersey because now you're playing for country."

During workouts before the Olympics, he got to know his teammates. He took every opportunity to display his leadership skills, setting an example as one of the first to show up at practice and one of the last to leave. Since Kobe had grown up overseas, when he told them how tough the other teams would be, his teammates listened. "It was important for me to impress upon them, 'Look, these international players can play,'" he said. To win the gold medal, every player would have to do what was best for the team.

After easily beating overmatched China and Greece, when Team USA faced Spain, one of the tournament favorites, Kobe set the tone as a team player. Early in the contest, as Kobe followed the player he was guarding out toward the three-point line, fellow Laker Pau Gasol, a member of the Spanish team, stood in his way, setting a screen.

But Kobe didn't back off. Gasol might have been a Laker, but now he was a member of the opposition. Kobe lowered his shoulder and sent Gasol tumbling backward. He was playing to win!

"I wanted to send Pau a message," he said later. "This is what you have to be willing to do in order to win titles. So, it was kind of a dual message, one for our team and USA and winning this game, winning this medal, but also for Pau in understanding this is the line that you have to cross in order to be a champion."

LeBron James said that at that moment he realized Kobe was "all about winning and whoever he's playing for or who he's playing with at that point in time. He really forgot Pau was his teammate." Team USA went on to roll over Spain 119–82. They went undefeated in group play, then dumped Australia and Argentina to face Spain once more in the gold medal game.

The two teams played each other evenly for most of the game. Kobe did what he had done in every other game; play good defense, rebound, and help distribute the ball to his teammates. So far in the Olympics, he hadn't really needed to score very much in order for Team USA to win. But now, with time running down, Kobe realized that it was time to be "all about winning." Spain wasn't guarding him very closely, and with time running out his team now needed him to score.

With only eight minutes left in the game, he went off, first driving down the lane and pulling up for a short jumper to give the United States a 93–89 lead. The next time down the court, he took the same route, only instead of taking the shot himself, he dished off to Deron Williams for a three-pointer. Then he fed Dwight Howard for a dunk. All of a sudden it was 98–89.

Kobe couldn't believe that Spain was still trying to cover him with a single player. He worked free for a wide-open three-pointer to make the score 101–92, and the game seemed to be over. But Spain didn't give up and drew to within five points of Team USA, trailing 104–99. Fortunately, Kobe didn't give up either. Team USA came flying down the court. Kobe set up just outside the three-point line, and Dwyane Wade hit him with a pass.

Kobe was wide open, but he hesitated for a fraction of a second, just enough time for the Spanish defender to think he could block Kobe's shot. Bryant went up and launched the three-pointer just before the defender's hand smacked into his arm. The ball dropped through the net and the referee blew the whistle, calling a foul and sending Kobe to the line. As the crowd roared, he put his finger to his lips as if to quiet them, to make sure everyone realized the game wasn't over. Then he calmly sank the free throw.

The four-point play sealed the victory, and the USA went on to win 118–107. As the TV broadcaster noted at the time, Kobe "came through when the United States needed him most."

"It's right up there at the top because of what's at stake," Kobe said later of the win. I still tease Pau about it. . . . I hadn't shot the ball all game and so the last two minutes I'm in single coverage."

At the medal ceremony, he proudly held his jersey out so everyone could see USA emblazoned on his chest. Only a few months before, the NBA season had ended as a nightmare, with people questioning his leadership. Now, with a gold medal around his neck, everything had changed.

Kobe hoped that now he'd be able to follow up on a gold medal with another NBA championship...or maybe two or three more!

★ CHAPTER EIGHTEEN ★

2009

Kobe's Team

Kobe and the Lakers entered the 2008–2009 season with something to prove. The loss to the Celtics in the Finals had stung. But Kobe carried the confidence he had gained during the Olympics into the regular season.

Helped out by the return of center Andrew Bynum, who had been hurt the previous season, the Lakers got off to a terrific start, winning their first seven games and beginning the season 21–3.

Kobe built on his Olympic performance and began to be recognized as one of the best all-around players in the league. Earlier in his career, he had sometimes struggled to fit in with his more experienced teammates. Now, as Michael Jordan had said, he had "figured it out" and emerged as a true leader, determined to provide whatever his team needed, whether it was a rebound to spark a fast break, a sweet pass for an assist, or a key bucket.

All year long the Lakers played as a team, on and off the court, all focused on the same goal. As Kobe later said, "That '08–09 team, I think that's the most fun I've ever had playing on a team. We hung out all day.... Just a fun season."

One of the most enjoyable games of the season came on February 2, 2009, at New York's Madison Square Garden against the New York Knicks, winners of their last five games. New York hoped to make a statement against the first-place Lakers.

Bryant was always excited to play in New York. The Knicks' home court, Madison Square Garden, is one of the most storied arenas in basketball, the site of many classic games in both professional and college hoops, and Bryant loved playing on the big stage. The Lakers needed him to have a big game. Bynum was out again with a minor injury, and Kobe knew he would have to pick up the slack.

During this game, Kobe looked to score. He took control early, popping free at the top of the key to score the Lakers' first bucket just a few seconds into the game, then following that with a long three-pointer. The game was only a few minutes old and it was clear that Kobe was on fire. Almost every trip down the court either resulted in a score by Kobe or, if the Knicks collapsed their defense on him, a pass to a teammate for a score. In the first five minutes, Bryant scored 11 points.

Fans in the stands began to wonder if they were about to witness a record performance. In the hundreds and hundreds of professional and college basketball games played at the Garden since it had opened in 1968, the most points ever scored in a game by an individual player were 60 points, set by Knicks great Bernard King on Christmas Day in 1984. The record high for an opposing player was 55, set by the great Michael Jordan in 1995. Kobe was on pace to shatter both records.

The Knicks tried everything, but they couldn't stop Kobe. If they played him loose, he calmly launched a deadly jump shot. If they tried to play him close, he drove to the basket. It looked like Kobe was playing at a faster speed than everyone else on the court.

By halftime he had 34 points. In the second half, as the Lakers took a comfortable lead, the only question became how many points Kobe would score.

As Kobe scored point after point, New York basketball fans realized they were seeing history in the making. They stopped cheering for the Knicks and started to cheer for Kobe.

Nothing the Knicks did could slow him down. With just under four minutes left in the game, Kobe had 54 points. One more would break Jordan's record. He got the ball just outside the three-point line, a Knicks defender draped all over him. Somehow, he still found a way to get off a shot, a twisting, one-handed three-pointer.

The referee blew the whistle as the shot fell short. Foul!

Bryant calmly stepped to the free throw line and drained all three shots to pass Jordan with 57 points. Could he now top Bernard King for the arena record?

A few moments later, Kobe drove down the middle of the court, and with a Knicks defender playing him tight, Bryant pulled up just outside the free throw line. There didn't seem to be any way for him to get off a shot and the passing lane was blocked.

Then, in a flash, he pump faked, the defender reached up...and Kobe spun quickly to his left, leaving the defender in the air and Kobe in the clear. He dropped in the short jump shot and the stands erupted in cheers. The television announcer burst out laughing, and sitting in his usual front-row seat, Knicks superfan film director Spike Lee jumped out of his chair and started laughing and shaking his head.

With only two minutes remaining, Kobe drove to the hoop one more time. Drawing a foul, he sank both free throws for the record of 61 points. Coach Phil Jackson pulled him from the game, and the entire crowd stood and cheered. The Lakers beat the Knicks 126–117. Kobe made nineteen of thirty-one shots during the game and sank all twenty free throws.

When a reporter told Kobe after the game that he had just set the Madison Square Garden record, he just started laughing. "I don't know that," he said, genuinely surprised. "That's awesome!" Then he pointed out that with Andrew Bynum hurt, the Lakers really needed the win. All he did, he said, "was read the defense…me scoring is a luxury, not a necessity." It was just something the team needed that day to win.

Even though he had set a record, he also knew that the season would not be a success unless he ended it with a championship. The Lakers entered the playoffs as favorites to win the title. In the first round they easily defeated Utah, and then beat Houston and Denver in two hard-fought series to reach the Finals against the Orlando Magic. Led by center Dwight Howard, the Magic had entered the playoffs as underdogs but then beat LeBron James's Cavaliers and the defending champion Celtics to reach the Finals.

Bryant and his teammates knew better than to underestimate the Magic. Kobe had seen what Dwight Howard could do during the Olympics, and in the regular season, the Magic had gone undefeated against Los Angeles.

Bryant responded with a completely dominant performance in the Finals. He didn't stand out for a particularly fabulous shot or a single great game—he was great for the entire series. In Game 1 he scored 40 points as Los Angeles overwhelmed the Magic, 100–75. Game 2 went to overtime, and in the final moments it was Kobe who made a key pass to Pau Gasol for an easy bucket to secure the win.

The Magic won Game 3, but Bryant and the Lakers would not be denied the title, taking the next two games to win the title. Kobe averaged 32.4 points and 7.4 assists for the series, the best combined performance in those two categories in the Finals since Lakers great Jerry West averaged 37.9 points and 7.4 assists in 1969. To no surprise, Kobe was named MVP.

For the moment, the memories of the humiliating defeat in Boston were washed away. When a reporter asked him what the difference was, Kobe said, "You grow as a person, you grow as a man and figure out the best way to lead these guys."

That's exactly what he had done. The championship was the fifteenth in Lakers history, and Bryant's fourth, but his first without Shaquille O'Neal. Although he and Shaq had long since buried their differences, Bryant later said that he "knew that when my career's over they're going to chastise me for the same thing: 'Oh well, you're only great because you played with Shaq'... I didn't want people to use that against me... it was important that I win championships without him."

There was no longer any question: the Lakers were his team, and their success depended on him.

★ CHAPTER NINETEEN ★

2010

Celtics Redemption

Kobe still wasn't satisfied. To be considered one of the NBA's all-time greats, he knew that four championships would not be enough. Some people still held the loss to the Celtics in the Finals against him. Before his career ended, he hoped to have the opportunity to face the Celtics in the Finals at least once more. This time, he was determined to win.

At first it seemed as if the Lakers would be even better in the 2009–2010 season. They signed free agent forward Ron Artest (who later changed his name to Metta World Peace), one of the best defensive players in the NBA. With Artest on board, the Lakers looked unbeatable.

And at first they were—winning seven of their eight games and soon following that with an eleven-game winning streak. Then, the injuries hit. First, Kobe broke a finger in his right hand. Although he continued to play, it still hampered his game. Then Artest suffered a concussion, and in February, Kobe sprained an ankle. After not missing a game since 2007, he was forced to sit out two weeks. Nevertheless, the Lakers still managed to make the playoffs.

Although the Boston Celtics had finished as the number four seed in the Eastern Conference, they easily beat the Heat and then the two teams with the best regular-season record, the Cavaliers and the Magic, to make the Finals. The Lakers took care of business, too, beating the Thunder, Jazz, and the Suns to earn the right to play Boston.

Everyone knew this was the matchup Kobe and the Lakers wanted. He had waited two long years to have another chance to win a championship over Boston.

After Game 1, the Lakers seemed likely to do just that as Bryant dropped in 30 points in an easy 102–89 win. But in Game 2 the Celtics' sharpshooter Ray Allen got hot, hitting eight of eleven three-point shots to lead the Celtics to a 104–93 victory. With 29 points, Kobe then led the Lakers to a win in Game 3, only to have the Celtics come roaring back to win the next two games. With the final two games scheduled on the Lakers' home court, all the Celtics needed was one more win to take the championship.

Sitting in the locker room, Kobe looked around at his teammates. They looked as if they had already lost. As the team's leader, he knew it was up to him to change their attitude. He didn't stand on his chair and start yelling. Instead, he started laughing! His teammates stared at him. What was so funny about losing a game in the Finals?

Then, as Kobe explained later, he told the team why he was laughing. "First of all," he said, "they kicked our butt. So that's pretty funny. And secondly, if we started the season and they told us that all we had to go do was go home and win two games to be NBA champions, would you take that deal?"

His teammates thought for a moment and agreed. As Bryant later told a reporter, "They said, 'Yeah we'd take that deal.'" Then Kobe explained, "Alright then, that's all we gotta do. Go home, win two games. That's it. Then we're NBA champions." Instead of thinking about what had gone wrong in the last two games, the Lakers started focusing on the next two games. Without scoring a point, Kobe had changed the attitude of the whole team.

In Game 6, they got a break. Early in the contest, Celtics center Kendrick Perkins injured his knee and had to leave the game. The Celtics struggled to adjust, and the Lakers clamped down on defense. They dominated the Celtics, leading by as many as 27 points, and rolled to an 89–67 win.

With the series now tied, it all came down to Game 7. This was the game that all basketball fans wanted to see, the NBA's two most legendary franchises, playing a single game with the championship on the line. And Kobe knew that if the Celtics won, everyone would say that, for all his accomplishments, a team led by Kobe Bryant in the end just could not beat the Celtics.

The game was a defensive struggle from the start, as both teams played hard and tough, challenging every shot. And both teams seemed a little tight, particularly the Lakers, who missed several easy shots early in the game. Even Kobe seemed affected. The pressure of Game 7 seemed to be getting to him, as shot after shot clanged off the rim or the glass. Fortunately, Ron Artest and Pau Gasol kept the Lakers in the game. Still, at halftime the Celtics led 40–34.

At the start of the second half, the Celtics came out on fire, going on a 9–2 run to open up a 49–36 lead. All of a sudden it looked as if Boston would win in a blowout, just as they had in 2008.

But Kobe Bryant was a different player in 2010. The gold medal and the 2009 championship had given him the confidence to play his best when he needed to. Coach Jackson called a time-out to slow the Celtics' run. Kobe knew it was up to him to give his team a spark.

Immediately after the time-out, Lamar Odom fed Kobe on the fly for a running jumper. *Swish*!

The crowd in Los Angeles sensed a change in momentum. By the end of the period, the Celtics' lead was down to four, 57–53. At the start of the fourth quarter, the Lakers' surge continued. Artest and Gasol controlled the inside, and Derek Fisher sank a three to knot the score at 64–64.

The next time down the court, Bryant was fouled and hit both shots. When the Lakers got the ball back, the game was in Kobe's hands. He had been cold all night. Another player might not have wanted the ball, afraid to fail. But Kobe knew it was his time to lead. From the three-point line, he started to drive, then pulled up, lifted the ball, pulled it back down, then launched a shot. Good! Now the Lakers led 68–64.

Still, the Celtics refused to give up and drew back to within three at 76–73. Then came the play of the game. With only one minute left, Kobe had the ball in the middle of the court, just outside the three-point line. Everyone in the arena expected him to shoot.

So did the Celtics. Ray Allen, guarding Kobe, pressed him close. Then Kobe, out of the corner of his eye, saw Ron Artest to his right, all alone far outside the three-point line. He lifted the ball as if to shoot but instead lofted it over to Artest.

The Celtics couldn't believe it. Although the defensive specialist had hit a three-pointer earlier in the game, Artest wasn't known as a three-point shooter. A defender raced over too late to stop his shot. Artest fired the ball toward the hoop.

Everyone held their breath as the improbable shot arced down toward the basket...and went in! The referee thrust both hands in the air to designate the three-pointer, and Kobe did the same, a look of surprise on this face. Now the Lakers led 79–73. In the final minute, Kobe hit two more free throws. When a last-second desperation shot by the Celtics fell short, Lamar Odom gathered the ball and threw it down the court. Kobe chased it down as the final buzzer sounded, giving the Lakers an 83–79 win. Then, cradling the basketball to his chest, he joined his teammates in a midcourt celebration. For the second year in a row, Kobe Bryant's Lakers were NBA champions!

Although he only made six of twenty-four shots in Game 7, he had made them when it counted, scoring 10 points in the fourth quarter. More importantly, he had made the big pass at the right time to win the game.

"He never passes me the ball, and he passed me the ball!" Artest joked after the game as if he could barely believe it. "Kobe passed me the ball, and I shot a three!"

As he sat at a press conference after the game with his daughters in his lap, Kobe said, "This one is by far the sweetest, because it's them," referring to the Celtics. "This was the hardest one by far. I wanted it so bad, and sometimes when you want it so bad, it slips away from you." He realized he never could have done it without his teammates. "My guys picked me up," he added.

The victory made it clear that Kobe Bryant was now one of the greatest NBA players in history. With five championship rings, he now had one more than Shaquille O'Neal, and was tied with Hall-of-Famers Kareem Abdul-Jabbar and George Mikan for the most in Lakers history.

To no surprise, for the second year in a row, he was named Finals MVP. That was nice, but not as nice as a fifth championship ring!

★ CHAPTER TWENTY ★

2011–2016

Winding Down

In the 2010–2011 season, Kobe and the Lakers looked forward to a third championship in a row, a "three-peat," something the team had not done since 1999–2002. But it was not to be. As Kobe pursued a sixth championship over the next few seasons, he and the Lakers would fall short.

They didn't fall apart; Kobe continued to perform at a very high level. Yet during each of the next few seasons, something would go wrong and prevent the Lakers from reaching the finals.

For much of the 2010–11 season, a trip to the finals seemed within reach, particularly after the Lakers went 17–1 after the All-Star break. But a short time before the playoffs, Andrew Bynum was lost to a suspension and then got hurt. Although he would return for the playoffs, the Lakers were thrown off stride and lost in the second round in four straight games to Dallas.

Coach Phil Jackson left the team at the end of the season and was replaced by Mike Brown for 2011–2012, but after a labor dispute cut the season to only sixty-six games, the Lakers never really got on track. They fell in the second round of the playoffs for the second year in a row, this time losing to Oklahoma City in five games.

It wasn't Kobe's fault, as he averaged over 25 points a game each season, and was named All-Star MVP in 2011. He didn't realize it at the time, but the loss to Oklahoma City would be his last appearance in the playoffs.

For Kobe, a return to the Olympics would be the highlight of the season. Surrounded by a host of talented teammates, including LeBron James, the team didn't depend on Kobe as much as they had in 2008. He still enjoyed a fine Olympics, picking up his second gold medal, and ending his career as an undefeated Olympian.

In 2012–2013, Kobe and the Lakers seemed certain to rebound back to title contention as they added All-Star center Dwight Howard and two-time MVP Steve Nash to the roster, but Coach Brown tried to change the team's offense. The new group struggled to learn the system and Brown was eventually fired.

Under new coach Mike D'Antoni, who had played in Italy and known Kobe when he was a child, the Lakers finally started playing well together.

Then, on April 12, 2013, disaster struck. With only three minutes remaining in a game against the Golden State Warriors, Kobe started to drive then fell to the ground, grimacing in pain, grabbing his left leg. His left Achilles tendon had torn. He had to be helped off the court. His season was over.

Many people thought the injury marked the end of Kobe's career. So did he. He was thirty-five years old and knew that Achilles injuries take a long time to heal.

He took to Facebook and wrote, "Do I have the consistent will to overcome this thing? Maybe I should break out the rocking chair and reminisce on the career that was. Maybe this is how my book ends. Maybe Father Time has defeated me."

Then he snapped out of it, telling himself in the same post, "Stop feeling sorry for yourself. Find the silver lining and get to work with the same belief, same drive and same conviction as ever."

Kobe had surgery and did just that. He worked long and hard in the off-season to rehabilitate his leg, all the while worrying if he would ever be as good as he had been before.

Sadly, the answer would be "no," or at least "not very often" and "not very soon." He returned to the lineup in December but then suffered a fracture in his left knee and missed another six weeks. Although he made it back onto the court after missing only a few games, it became obvious that he wasn't ready to play. When his season ended, he'd appeared in only six games.

After another long off-season trying to regain his health, he returned to the court for the 2014–15 season. Although he passed Michael Jordan to become the third leading scorer in NBA history, he wasn't quite the same. While still a dangerous player when healthy, he wasn't healthy very often. At various times his back, knees, feet, and Achilles all started giving him trouble. Then in January he suffered an injury to his shoulder. After playing only thirty-five games and averaging 22 points a game, he had to have surgery.

But "Father Time" hadn't beaten him yet. He worked out hard in the off-season, determined to play again. Yet as the 2015–16 season began, he knew it would soon be time to retire. He had played the game since he was a little boy growing up in Italy and was now in his twentieth season in the NBA. At age thirty-seven, his body was wearing out.

All the time he had spent away from basketball

the past few years made him realize just how much he loved the game, and he wanted to express that to others. He approached *The Player's Tribune*, a website founded by former New York Yankees shortstop Derek Jeter, to publish a poem he had written to announce his retirement and explain just how much the game meant to him.

The poem, written as a letter to the game, was published on November 29, 2015, and titled "Dear Basketball." In it, Kobe began by remembering how, as a six-year-old, he had rolled up his father's tube socks and taken "imaginary, game winning shots" into a trash can. He soon fell in love with the game, "A love so deep I gave you my all." He played not because he had to, but because, somehow, the game seemed to want him to play.

At the end of the poem, he announced his retirement and said that despite all his achievements and struggles, he still loved the game as much as he did when he was a young boy. He ended the poem simply: "Love you always."

For Kobe, basketball wasn't just about winning, or making money and becoming famous. It was about giving all he had to something else, to become the best he could be.

Fans and players alike responded to the poem. They recognized the love they had for the game in the words that Kobe wrote.

Although Kobe wanted to leave the game with another championship, the Lakers were rebuilding with younger players. They struggled to win all year.

Kobe struggled as well. At times it seemed as if he had played one year too long, although every once in a while he would manage to turn back the clock, as he did in a February game against Minnesota, when he scored 38 points, including 7 three-pointers. He ended up averaging only a little more than 17 points a game, yet he was still the leading vote-getter for the 2016 All-Star team, a sign of just how much he meant to basketball fans. Although Kobe didn't want other teams in the league to hold any ceremonies honoring him, many did anyway, playing special video tributes before his final appearance in each city. Fans who had once rooted against him now stood and cheered. He played his last NBA game on April 13, 2016.

Before the game started, the Lakers held a long ceremony that featured several commemorative high-light videos, including tributes from former team-mates like Shaq and opponents like Dirk Nowitzki.

After such an emotional experience, no one expected much of a game from Kobe.

And at first, he didn't give them one. In the first quarter, shot after shot clanged off the rim as he missed his first five baskets. "I had a little bit of nerves," he said later.

Earlier in his career, Kobe had adopted the nickname "Mamba" from a character in an action film to help him focus on the court. A large venomous snake, the mamba is known for its ability to strike quickly and is very dangerous. "When I step on that court, I become that," he said. "I am that killer snake. I'm stone cold, man." It fit his style of play perfectly.

All of a sudden, the Mamba returned. It was as if the game of basketball decided to give him a going-away gift. For one last time, he would be the best player on the court.

It started with a drive down the lane, a fake, and a long, high, arcing floater that one sportswriter called a "crescent moon shot." That broke the ice, and he went on to drain his next four shots.

Now it seemed as if he was the only player on the court. His teammates kept feeding him the ball and Kobe kept shooting. He finished the first quarter with 22 points on an incredible twenty shots.

Even though his scoring pace slowed in the second and third quarters, the game was close, and in the fourth quarter Kobe was determined to go out as a winner.

His teammates kept feeding him the ball and Kobe kept scoring; twisting drives down the lane, soaring three-pointers, and simple pull-up jump shots, it didn't matter. The Jazz were playing him tough, but Kobe could not be stopped. With each point the crowd got louder. Chants of "MVP! MVP!" rained down from the stands.

Still, with just over thirty seconds remaining, the Lakers trailed 96–95. Kobe took the ball up the court, started toward the basket, then pulled up and took the last jump shot of his career.

Swish! The basket gave Bryant 58 points for the game and gave the Lakers a 97–95 lead.

Kobe stayed in the game, and with the score 97–96, he got the ball one last time. He was fouled before he could take a shot. Then, as he had thousands of times before, he calmly sank first one foul shot, then the next, his final two points. Incredibly, he had scored 60 points.

But he still wasn't done. With only seconds left to play, Kobe got the ball under the Utah basket. Still playing to win, he spotted a teammate far down court and threw him the ball for a thunderous dunk to secure the 101–96 victory. Utah called time-out, and with four seconds remaining, Kobe Bryant walked off the court as a player for the last time. Not only had he scored 60 points, but in the fourth quarter, he outscored the entire Jazz team all by himself, 23–21. And the Lakers had won!

Even Kobe could barely believe what had just taken place. "I can't believe this is happening. This is crazy to me. It's crazy to me," Bryant said after the game. "I'm just deeply honored by the fans, to be able to put on that type of show for them after all the support they've given me. We grew up together."

It may not have been a championship, but for Lakers fans who had grown up with Kobe, it was unforgettable.

★ CHAPTER TWENTY-ONE ★

2017 and Beyond

Legacy

At the time of his retirement, there was no question that Kobe Bryant was one of the greatest basketball players of all time. In addition to his five titles, he ended his career with eighteen All-Star appearances, four All-Star Game MVP awards, a regular season MVP award, and two Finals MVP awards. In his twenty-year NBA career, he averaged 25.0 points, 5.2 rebounds, 4.7 assists, and 1.4 steals per game.

But there was always more to Kobe Bryant than basketball. It was time to give back, explore other interests, and help his wife, Vanessa, raise their daughters. Kobe and Vanessa raised money for a number of different charities, including his own foundation. In 2018, he wrote a book, *The Mamba Mentality: How I Play*, a collection of his thoughts on basketball illustrated with photographs. A couple years later, he continued his writing career and published The

Wizenard series for kids, which combined basketball with a little bit of magic.

Inspired by the public's reaction to "Dear Basketball," Bryant decided to make an animated film of the same name. He opened a studio and put together a team of award-winning animators, designers, and composers to bring the story to life. The result was a film of just over five minutes featuring Bryant's words and his narration.

Fans loved it. So did the critics and other filmmakers. In 2018, Bryant received an Oscar, an Academy Award for Best Animated Short Film, becoming the first former professional athlete ever to win the award. Kobe called it a "tremendous honor" and was very proud to be recognized for an achievement outside of basketball. "As basketball players we're supposed to shut up and dribble," he said, "but we do a little more than that."

Now, Kobe was a father first. He and Vanessa already had two daughters, Natalia and Gianna (known as GiGi). Another daughter, Bianka, was born soon after he retired, and a fourth daughter, Capri, was born in 2019. With a house full of girls, Kobe supported his daughters in whatever they wanted to do.

Shortly after Kobe retired, GiGi got the basketball

bug. She was just like young Kobe, shooting tube socks into the trash can.

He soon found himself giving GiGi pointers and watching games with her. Although Bryant had never expressed any interest in coaching, he opened Mamba Sports Academy and started coaching GiGi's team. Fans became accustomed to seeing GiGi at her father's side as they watched basketball together. She would watch intently as he pointed to the court and gave her tips.

Kobe saw a lot of himself in his daughter. She already knew what she wanted to do with the rest of her life. She told him her dream was to play on the basketball team at the University of Connecticut and then go on to a career in the WNBA. As Kobe told one television interviewer, "The best thing that happens is when we go out, and fans will come up to me and she'll be standing next to me and they'll be like, 'You gotta have a boy, have somebody to carry on the tradition,'" just as Kobe had carried on the tradition from his father. Then, Kobe told the interviewer, GiGi would speak up. She was determined to fulfill her father's legacy herself and become the next great Bryant to play basketball. "No boy for that," she would say. "I got this."

On January 25, 2020, LeBron James passed Kobe to become the third-highest scorer in NBA history with 33,655 points. Bryant congratulated James on Twitter. "Continuing to move the game forward @KingJames," he tweeted. "Much respect my brother." The respect was mutual. In fact, when James took to the court that night, he wrote *Mamba$ Life* in Kobe's honor on one of his sneakers.

Early the next morning, a Sunday, Kobe Bryant got up early to go to church and then went back home to pick up GiGi. Her squad, Team Mamba, was playing in a tournament at his academy. Rather than drive to the tournament, Kobe and GiGi planned to take a helicopter. Kobe invited several other players and their parents to join them on the flight.

At around 9:45 a.m., the helicopter lost control and crashed into a hillside. Tragically, Kobe, GiGi, and the other seven passengers were killed.

The sports world was stunned. It did not seem possible that Kobe Bryant, a player fans had watched grow up in the NBA, was gone.

Many learned about his death while showing up to attend NBA games later that day. Fans gathered at Kobe's home court, the Staples Center, in tears, bearing flowers. Teams held special tributes, and many NBA players found their own way to honor Kobe—who over the past several years had served as a role model and mentor for the next generation of NBA stars. The Celtics and Pelicans, playing in New Orleans, purposely took twenty-four-second shot clock violations at the start of their games in honor of Bryant, who had played under the jersey numbers 8 and 24. Others wrote tributes to Kobe and his daughter on their sneakers.

His old teammates could not believe it. In a message posted on Twitter, Shaquille O'Neal said there were "no words to express the pain...My condolences goes out to the Bryant family and the families of the other passengers on board." Magic Johnson posted, "Laker Nation, the game of basketball & our city, will never be the same without Kobe." Kareem Abdul-Jabbar made a video for Twitter. Wearing a purple Lakers sweatshirt, he said, "Most people will remember Kobe as the magnificent athlete who inspired a whole generation of basketball players. But I will always remember him as a man who was much more than an athlete." Michael Jordan added, "Words can't describe the pain I'm feeling. I loved Kobe—he was like a little brother to me."

NBA Commissioner Adam Silver called Kobe "one

of the most extraordinary players in the history of our game...he will be remembered most for inspiring people around the world to pick up a basketball and compete to the very best of their ability."

It was sad that he was gone, and sadder still that Bryant was no longer able to add to his legacy. President Barack Obama said, "Kobe was a legend on the court and just getting started in what would have been just as meaningful a second act."

He will never be forgotten. In videos, Kobe still plays on, still makes amazing plays, and still leads his team. As long as the game of basketball is played and the greatest players are remembered, Kobe Bryant's name will be mentioned, not just for what he did on the court, but for how much he meant to the game and how much he loved basketball.

As he said at the end of his farewell speech:
"Mamba out."

Kobe Bryant's Career Highlights

USA Today's High School Player of the Year, 1996

Youngest player to start an NBA game (January 28, 1997, against Dallas Mavericks)

NBA Slam Dunk Champion and Rookie All-Star Game MVP, 1997

Youngest player to start an All-Star Game, 1998

Five-time NBA Champion, winning the title in 2000, 2001, 2002, 2009, and 2010

NBA Scoring Champion in 2006 and 2007

NBA Most Valuable Player in 2008

NBA Finals Most Valuable Player in 2009 and 2010

NBA All-Star Game MVP four times (2002, 2007, 2009, 2011)

NBA All-Defensive First Team nine times (2000, 2003, 2004, 2006–2011)

Two-time United States Olympic Gold Medalist in 2008 and 2012

All-NBA First Team eleven times (2002–2004, 2006–2013)

Eighteen-time NBA All-Star (1998, 2000–2016)

All-Time Lakers leading scorer with 33,643 points and fourth in the NBA all-time

Winner of an Academy Award for Best Animated Short Film in 2018

Kobe Bryant Career Statistics

Season	TEAM	GP	GS	MIN	FG%	3P%	FT%	OREB	DREB	REB	APG	SPG	BPG	TO	PF	PTS
1996–97	LAL	71	6	15.5	41.7	37.5	81.9	0.7	1.2	1.9	1.3	0.7	0.3	1.6	1.4	7.6
1997–98	LAL	79	1	26.0	42.8	34.1	79.4	1.0	2.1	3.1	2.5	0.9	0.5	2.0	2.3	15.4
1998–99	LAL	50	50	37.9	46.5	26.7	83.9	1.1	4.2	5.3	3.8	1.4	1.0	3.1	3.1	19.9
1999–00	LAL	66	62	38.2	46.8	31.9	82.1	1.6	4.7	6.3	4.9	1.6	0.9	2.8	3.3	22.5
2000–01	LAL	68	68	40.9	46.4	30.5	85.3	1.5	4.3	5.9	5.0	1.7	0.6	3.2	3.3	28.5
2001–02	LAL	80	80	38.3	46.9	25.0	82.9	1.4	4.1	5.5	5.5	1.5	0.4	2.8	2.9	25.2
2002–03	LAL	82	82	41.5	45.1	38.3	84.3	1.3	5.6	6.9	5.9	2.2	0.8	3.5	2.7	30.0
2003–04	LAL	65	64	37.6	43.8	32.7	85.2	1.6	3.9	5.5	5.1	1.7	0.4	2.6	2.7	24.0
2004–05	LAL	66	66	40.7	43.3	33.9	81.6	1.4	4.5	5.9	6.0	1.3	0.8	4.1	2.6	27.6
2005–06	LAL	80	80	41.0	45.0	34.7	85.0	0.9	4.4	5.3	4.5	1.8	0.4	3.1	2.9	35.4
2006–07	LAL	77	77	40.8	46.3	34.4	86.8	1.0	4.7	5.7	5.4	1.4	0.5	3.3	2.7	31.6
2007–08	LAL	82	82	38.9	45.9	36.1	84.0	1.1	5.2	6.3	5.4	1.8	0.5	3.1	2.8	28.3
2008–09	LAL	82	82	36.1	46.7	35.1	85.6	1.1	4.1	5.2	4.9	1.5	0.5	2.6	2.3	26.8
2009–10	LAL	73	73	38.8	45.6	32.9	81.1	1.1	4.3	5.4	5.0	1.5	0.3	3.2	2.6	27.0
2010–11	LAL	82	82	33.9	45.1	32.3	82.8	1.0	4.1	5.1	4.7	1.2	0.1	3.0	2.1	25.3
2011–12	LAL	58	58	38.5	43.0	30.3	84.5	1.1	4.3	5.4	4.6	1.2	0.3	3.5	1.8	27.9
2012–13	LAL	78	78	38.6	46.3	32.4	83.9	0.8	4.7	5.6	6.0	1.4	0.3	3.7	2.2	27.3
2013–14	LAL	6	6	29.5	42.5	18.8	85.7	0.3	4.0	4.3	6.3	1.2	0.2	5.7	1.5	13.8
2014–15	LAL	35	35	34.5	37.3	29.3	81.3	0.7	4.9	5.7	5.6	1.3	0.2	3.7	1.9	22.3
2015–16	LAL	66	66	28.2	35.8	28.5	82.6	0.6	3.1	3.7	2.8	0.9	0.2	2.0	1.7	17.6
Career		1,346	1,198	36.1	44.7	32.9	83.7	1.1	4.1	5.2	4.7	1.4	0.5	3.0	2.5	25.0
Postseason		220	200	39.3	44.8	33.1	81.6	1.0	4.0	5.1	4.7	1.4	0.7	2.9	3.0	25.6

GET ON THE FIELD, UNDER THE NET, AND BEHIND THE PLATE WITH YOUR FAVORITE ALL-STARS!

GREAT AMERICANS IN SPORTS
BABE RUTH
MATT CHRISTOPHER

GREAT AMERICANS IN SPORTS
MIA HAMM
MATT CHRISTOPHER

GREAT AMERICANS IN SPORTS
DREW BREES
MATT CHRISTOPHER

GREAT AMERICANS IN SPORTS
BLAKE GRIFFIN
MATT CHRISTOPHER

Read the entire *Great Americans in Sports* series by
MATT CHRISTOPHER

LB LITTLE, BROWN AND COMPANY
BOOKS FOR YOUNG READERS

LB-KIDS.COM

TWO PLAYERS, ONE DREAM...
to win the Little League Baseball® World Series

Read all about Carter's and Liam's journeys in the Little League series by MATT CHRISTOPHER.

 LITTLE, BROWN AND COMPANY
BOOKS FOR YOUNG READERS

Discover more at lb-kids.com